The
Senior
Texan
Legal Guide

By Paul Premack, Attorney at Law

Sterling Solutions
Bulverde, Texas

Distributed by **Sterling Solutions**
34296 U.S. Highway 281 North
Bulverde, Texas 78163

NOTICE: This book is intended to provide valuable information on its content topics. It is not, however, intended to replace individualized legal representation. If you have a specific legal situation, use this book to gain background knowledge. Seek further legal advice from your attorney.

Laws Change. The Author and Publisher of this book make every effort to keep its contents timely and up-to-date. But the law changes constantly. Please consult your legal advisor before you take action on any topic discussed in this book.

Gender. Many references in this book are in the male gender... "he," "him," "his," merely to simplify phrasing. Most concepts in this text apply generally to both males and females regardless of the gender mentioned.

ISBN: 0-945701-24-1
Library of Congress: LC 91-067324

I gratefully acknowledge the encouragement and contributions of my wife Ruthie S. Premack. Without her assistance, this book would not exist.

Thank you, Ruthie.

Printed on Recycled Paper

Introduction

Chapter 1: Medical Consent

Chapter 2: Artificial Life Support

Chapter 3: Health Care Powers of Attorney

Chapter 4: Rights of the Elderly

Chapter 5: Wills

Chapter 11: Powers of Attorney

Chapter 12: Living Trusts

Chapter 13: Gifts and Charitable Giving

Chapter 14: Guardianship

Introduction

While the information contained in this book is primarily aimed at the Senior Citizens of Texas, it will also provide valuable guidance and information for care providers, family members, and to everyone about to reach Senior status.

In the ideal world, all elderly people would remain healthy and vigorous throughout life. In the real world, a variety of crises may impose themselves into your "golden years." Careful planning is the key to retaining control over those years.

Planning should be attempted only after you gain full knowledge of your alternatives. This book is designed to provide that knowledge, and it is your duty to use the knowledge you gain from it. The benefits of careful planning will become clear as you read about the challenges that may lie ahead. Solutions *are* available; but you must *act* to benefit from them.

I have based this book on real-life examples from my private legal practice and on the hundreds of letters I have answered in my weekly newspaper column. The book is focused around answering your most pressing questions about the legalities of growing old: health care, estate planning, living trusts, asset management, family relations, banking, probate avoidance, and more.

So tell your friends about this book. Its information is hard to find elsewhere. Above all, read it carefully, learn about your alternatives, and plan wisely your own course of action.

Paul Premack
Fall, 1991

Chapter 1: Medical Consent

Informed Consent

In 1914, Judge Benjamin Cardozo (who eventually sat on the U.S. Supreme Court) voiced the principle of medical consent laws:

"Every human being of adult years and sound mind has a right to determine what shall be done with his own body."

All competent adults do have the right to make their own medical decisions. But to be valid, consent must be "informed" -- that is, given only after full disclosure to the decision maker of the risks and benefits of any proposed medical treatment.

1

Frequent medical malpractice claims have made health care providers wary of acting without proper consent. A patient, operated on without his consent, may charge the caregiver with negligence or even "battery" (unlawful physical contact).

When a person is not competent and is ill, who makes medical decisions? It is widely believed that spouses may give consent for surgery or other medical care for each other. In Texas, however, that is not true and caregivers are moving away from the practice.

Exceptions to the Rule

Unless you have made other arrangements, two medical situations do not require your explicit prior consent:

- First, if you are unable to communicate and your life is threatened by injury or illness, law allows your caregiver to presume you give consent to medical care.

- Second, medical care is allowed without consent if your doctor says the benefits of therapy would be reduced if the therapy was explained in detail.

Default Answer: Guardianship

If no other plans were made in advance, then caregivers may insist on a legal guardianship when seeking authorized consent for medical treatment. Guardianship is expensive. Guardianship is also court supervised. But for a person who has not pre-planned, guardianship may be the only option.

Your *planning alternatives* to avoid guardianship are:

- appointing an Agent (with a proper health care Power of Attorney) to give consent for you, without court intervention; (*see* **Appendix A**)

- having a proper Natural Death Directive, which tells caregivers not to use machines to keep you alive if you have a terminal condition; and

- signing a declaration of guardian to specify who might become your guardian if an overprotective relative forces involuntary guardianship upon you.

Setting up advance instructions in this way can avoid court-appointed guardianship and ensure your control over uninterrupted medical care.

Chapter 2: Artificial Life Support

Documentation

The view that life should not be artificially sustained when there is no hope of normal life has become widely accepted in the last decade. Many people cringe at the thought of being hooked to life support machines, sustained after their time has passed.

A "Directive to Physicians" helps you avoid the emotional and monetary cost of lingering death, but (contrary to popular belief) a "living will" is a false and unenforceable promise of help. **Do not rely on a living will.** If you have one, it is not enforceable. Your should replace your "Living Will" with a "Directive to Physicians."

A "living will" is broad, usually stating that "if there is no reasonable expectation that I will recover..." from an illness, that "it is my wish that I be allowed to die without use of HEROIC MEASURES." Although that is an apparently clear expression of intent, a living will alone cannot guarantee your wishes will be followed.

The Texas "Directive to Physicians" is your instruction to remove artificial life support when death is imminent (or might occur within a relatively short time) because of a terminal condition. You must sign your Directive in front of two qualified witnesses.

The Texas Natural Death Act says you must have a "terminal condition" before life support can be removed. Two physicians (one of whom may be your primary care physician) must concur in the diagnosis. The doctors must continue to provide comfort and relieve pain.

The goal of our state's law is to allow death to come naturally: no sooner, no later. Texas does not allow any deliberate act to end a life.

Your physician must comply with the Directive. If he refuses, your doctor must transfer your care to another physician. Your physicians, nurses, and health care facilities are not subject to civil liability unless negligent. They may not be accused of any criminal act or of unprofessional conduct unless they are clearly negligent.

The technical requirements of this Act far remove it from the realm of simple "living wills." Death with dignity is possible. If freedom from machines and artificial intervention is your preference, you must replace your "living will" with a "Natural Death Directive."

Sample "Living Will"

Note: What follows is the UNENFORCEABLE document. This sample is provided so you will be able to recognize and REJECT this document!

To My Family, My Physician, My Lawyer and All Others Whom It May Concern:

Death is as much a reality as birth, growth, maturity and old age -- it is the one certainty of life. If the time comes when I can no longer take part in decisions for my own future, let this statement stand as an expression of my wishes and directions, while I am still of sound mind.

If at such a time the situation should arise in which there is no reasonable expectation of my recovery from extreme physical or mental disability, I direct that I be allowed to die and not be kept alive by medications, artificial means or "heroic measures."

This statement is made after careful consideration and is in accordance with my strong convictions and beliefs. I want the wishes and directions here expressed carried out to the extent permitted by law. Insofar as they are not legally enforceable, I hope that those to whom this Will is addressed will regard themselves as morally bound by these provisions.

Signed: Sam Citizen

Natural Death Directive

Sample Natural Death Directive

The following document is VALID and ENFORCEABLE. It is the one you should be using.

Directive to Physicians
Pursuant to Texas Health and Safety Code

Directive made on January 1, 1992.

I, Susan Citizen, being of sound mind, willfully and voluntarily make known my desire that my life shall not be artificially prolonged under the circumstances set forth below, and I declare that:

1. If at any time I should have an incurable condition caused by injury, disease, or illness certified to be a terminal condition by two physicians, and where the application of life sustaining procedures would serve only to artificially prolong the moment of my death and where my attending physician determines that my death is imminent or will result within a relatively short time without application of life sustaining procedures, I direct that such procedures be withheld or withdrawn, and that I be permitted to die naturally.

2. In the absence of my ability to give directions regarding the use of such life sustaining procedures, it is my intention that this directive shall be honored by my family and physicians as the final expression of my legal right to refuse medical or surgical treatment and accept the consequences from such refusal.

continued....

---

3. If I have been diagnosed as pregnant and that diagnosis is known to my Physician, this directive shall have no force or effect during the course of my pregnancy.

4. This directive shall be in effect until it is revoked.

5. I understand the full import of this directive and I am emotionally and mentally competent to make this directive.

6. I understand that I may revoke this directive at any time.

Signed: Susan Citizen, Declarant
Austin, Travis County, Texas

I am not related to the Declarant by blood or marriage; nor would I be entitled to any portion of the Declarant's Estate on her death; nor am I the attending Physician of Declarant or an employee of the attending Physician; nor am I a patient in the health care facility in which the Declarant is a patient, or any person who has a claim against any portion of the Estate of the Declarant upon her death. Furthermore, if I am an employee of a health facility in which the declarant is a patient, I am not involved in providing direct patient care to the declarant nor am I directly involved in the financial affairs of the health facility.

_____   _____
Witness   Witness

Note: This Directive to Physicians is appropriate for a woman. Obviously, paragraph 3 regarding pregnancy should be omitted from a male's Directive.

U.S. Supreme Court's Natural Death Decision

In the United States, we have a constitutional right to privacy and to a minimum amount of government intrusion into our lives, right?

In December 1989, the United States Supreme Court heard legal arguments in the *Cruzan v. State of Missouri* case. This case has had tremendous impact on the way in which we may exercise control over our own destinies.

History

In 1983, Nancy Cruzan was in an auto accident. Emergency personnel restored her pulse and respiration, though she had been without oxygen for 12 - 14 minutes. Before her condition was understood, the family consented to a feeding tube.

Although Cruzan has since died, she lived in a "persistent vegetative state" with only autonomic brain activity for about 8 years. She had neither a "living will" nor a "Natural Death Directive."

In 1987, Cruzan's family asked the Missouri Probate Court to allow removal of the feeding tube. They understood she would die if it was removed.

The Probate Court allowed removal, but Missouri appealed. The Missouri Supreme Court ordered the tube to remain, saying "the burdens of her treatment are not excessive to her." The Court decided that her right to refuse treatment was outweighed by the State's right to preserve life. The State kept this vegetative person alive, allowing her medical bills to accumulate, though the family wished otherwise.

The Missouri Supreme Court limited its decision to those persons without a "living will," the implication being that if Nancy had made a living will (in Texas, a "Natural Death Directive") the Court would have allowed the tube to be removed.

Court Arguments

Before the U.S. Supreme Court, the government argued it has an "absolute interest" in preserving life, and that to exercise this right it need only provide the citizen with adequate "due process." Once this courtesy is provided, the government should be able to impose its will on the citizen regardless of the citizen's wishes.

The Cruzan family, following a series of existing U.S. Supreme Court decisions, countered that the Constitution gives us each the right to privacy. The government cannot interfere with our decisions unless there is a "compelling state interest." They argued that there was no such compelling state interest in preserving the life of their comatose daughter.

The U.S. Supreme Court announced its decision in June 1990. It issued a very narrow holding -- no grand pronouncement of new rights nor an extinguishment of old ones: The Court said it is constitutional for a state to pass a law regulating the right to die.

Applied to Nancy Cruzan, this decision meant she had to stay on life support. She was later removed from life support because her family went back and complied with Missouri's state law, and she subsequently died.

Impact on Texans

Because of this Court decision, if you want to enforce your wishes to stay off life support equipment you must follow Texas law to the letter. This means the 1977 Natural Death Act must be your guide. You cannot use an informal "living will."

The Natural Death Act mandates use of the "Directive to Physicians" -- the form reprinted on pages 9 and 10. You cannot rely upon the "Living Will" since it is not based upon the Natural Death Act.

If you have one, tear up your Living Will and replace it with a Directive to Physicians.

Natural Death Directive instead of a Living Will

Chapter 3: Health Care Powers of Attorney

1989 Law

For each of us, the possibility of future sickness is a hurdle to be faced. None seem so high as those faced by an elderly ill person. There are some things you can do to help yourself and your family clear those hurdles.

The elderly, the largest consumers of medical care and the fastest growing segment in our population, bear a high risk of incapacity from a wide range of physical causes. A 1982 study established that approximately 17 out of 100 people over age 80 suffer significant loss of physical or mental abilities.

However, the once-common practice of allowing an un-qualified spouse or family member to provide consent if the patient cannot is declining. Hospital and doctor fear of lawsuits is eliminating unauthorized consent.

The 1989 "Durable Power of Attorney for Health Care" law allows you to appoint an agent to make health care decisions for you if you become unable to make those decisions for yourself. The appointment must be written in a format specified by the law. Using your own words is not enough. *See* **Appendix A** for a sample document.

You must sign the Power of Attorney in the presence of two qualified witnesses. Before signing, you must read and sign a disclosure form, stating you are aware the powers you are granting are very broad.

Who can be Agent?

Your Agent may be almost anyone you chose. Your Agent is powerless until your doctor certifies you have become incapable of understanding the nature and conse-quences of a needed health care decision.

When your agent makes a decision for you, he must act in the way you would have wanted, and must consider your religious beliefs, if known. If unknown, he must do what is in your "best interest." Control, ultimately, re-mains with you: even though certified as unable to de-cide, you must be informed of a health care decision in advance and may veto any proposed treatment.

Your agent can allow almost any treatment you could allow, unless you include specific limitations. Your Agent cannot deny "comfort care" under any condition.

Your Agent is not responsible for paying the bill for the care chosen. Decision-makers need not pay for a relative's medical care, unless they choose to. But without the Power of Attorney, payment might be due from anyone involved in the decision-making.

If the idea of delegating health care decision-making is new to you, you should discuss the matter with your family doctor and also seek expert legal advice. Plans must be made while you are healthy. Waiting "until later" may deny you the right to control your destiny.

Military Question: **I am retired military, and receive most of my health care needs on-base. Will the military doctors accept a Texas Health Care Power of Attorney?**

Answer:

Yes. Military policy calls for compliance with the protections afforded by state law. But note: there is a difference between policy and law. At a Military or Veterans facility, the staff is subject only to federal law and regulations and to military policy and regulations. Although currently honored, state law may be disregarded by the military if their internal policies change.

Chapter 4: Rights of the Elderly

Texas Law

Since 1983, Texas law has included a Bill of Rights for the elderly, which this law defines as anyone over age 55 (although many people over 55 don't consider themselves elderly).

The Bill of Rights comes into play when you are receiving any type of medical care. It is targeted at educating patients and caregivers about the level of care you should expect to receive. A caregiver may not deny an elderly individual a guaranteed right.

The Texas Department of Human Services oversees caregivers who receive funds from the Department.

Here is a list of your most important rights:

- ◆ You have the right to be treated with respect, consideration and recognition of your dignity and individuality. You have the right to receive personal care and private treatment.

- ◆ You have the right to be free from physical or chemical restraints unless there is an emergency and restraint is needed to protect you or others. Also, restraint is allowed for a limited time if authorized in writing by your doctor.

- ◆ You have a right to appropriate medical care regardless of your race, religion, color, national origin, sex, age, handicap, marital status, or the source of payment.

- ◆ You have a right to communicate with other people (in order to get medical care) in your native language.

- ◆ You have a right to voice your grievances and to recommend policy changes to your caregiver without fear of restraint, interference or reprisals.

- ◆ You have the right to choose your own personal physician.

- ◆ You have the right to associate and communicate with other individuals privately, unless your actions interfere with the rights of others.

♦ You have the right to inspect your medical records and to have them kept confidential by the caregiver. Records may only be released with your written permission.

♦ You have the right to be free from physical or mental abuse and exploitation by caregivers. Abuse involves intentional injury, unreasonable confinement and intimidation. Exploitation occurs when a caregiver uses your resources improperly for the caregiver's benefit.

Department of Veterans Affairs

The Department of Veterans Affairs hospitals provide medical care to thousands of patients, both elderly and younger. Title 38 of the Code of Federal Regulations includes an extensive listing of the medical rights of veterans while in a DVA hospital or facility.

Military: **Many retired military personnel are entitled to medical care at VA facilities. If you are treated there, you are entitled to protection of your rights.**

The Federal Regulations give all VA patients a right to be treated with dignity in a humane environment that affords them both reasonable protection from harm and appropriate privacy with regard to their personal needs.

All VA patients retain their legal rights, whether voluntarily or involuntarily admitted. These rights include:

- ◆ The right to hold and to dispose of property;

- ◆ The right to execute legal instruments, like a Will or Power of Attorney;

- ◆ The right to register and to vote;

- ◆ The right to refuse visitors;

- ◆ The right to freedom of worship. Regulations state that "No patient will be coerced into engaging in any religious activities against his or her desires."

- ◆ The right to be free from physical restraint or seclusion. This can be restricted when there is a risk that the patient may harm himself or others. Restraint or seclusion may not last longer than twenty-four hours without physician review.

- ◆ The right to be free from unnecessary or excessive medication.

Certain privileges can be suspended for VA patients when their doctor determines that exercise of a privilege might:

- harm the patient's physical or mental health, or

- stigmatize the patient's reputation to a degree that would adversely affect the patient's return to independent living, or

- infringe upon the rights of or jeopardize the health or safety of others, or

- adversely impact the operation of the medical facility.

All restricting orders must be reviewed at least once every 30 days by the practitioner and must be concurred in by the Chief of Service or Chief of Staff.

Like the Texas law requirement, the VA also requires that upon admission, a patient shall be informed of his rights.

Adult Protective Services

 Adult Protective Services
1-800-252-5400

Abuse and exploitation of a person over age 65 or a younger person who is disabled can be reported to Texas Adult Protective Services at 1-800-252-5400.

I was contacted by a 66-year-old widow who was under extreme stress. Her home had been broken into, and her property stolen multiple times. She had been beaten. She lived in fear of opening the door. Her drug-addicted son was responsible.

What can you do when confronted with that type of abuse? If you are a witness, you have a legal obligation to report the events to Adult Protective Services of the Texas Department of Human Services. All reports are confidential and state law provides immunity from potential civil or criminal liability arising out of your report.

Texas created Adult Protective Services (APS) in 1981. Since then, its case workers have handled an average of 2000 reports each month.

Definitions

About 60% of its cases involve "neglect," where an elderly person is without the goods or services necessary to prevent physical harm, mental anguish or mental illness even though there is a responsible caretaker.

Another 20% of APS cases involve reports of "abuse" involving intentional injury, unreasonable confinement, intimidation, or cruel punishment.

The rest deal with "exploitation" through illegal or improper acts of a caretaker who uses the elderly person's resources for the caretaker's personal benefit.

Protective services are available to anyone 65 or older or to anyone over 18 who has a mental, physical or developmental disability. The definition of "disability" is liberal, so if you are not sure whether a person qualifies, it is best to call anyway. APS' mission is to protect these persons from abuse, neglect and exploitation.

Upon receiving a report, APS is required to investigate within 24 hours. If it determines the elderly person really needs protection, APS then determines what services are needed, how the services will be paid for and if the elderly person wants the services.

Ability to Act

Adult Protective Services has been given by state law the tools it needs to act. With prior court authorization, it can enter a home (along with a police officer) to conduct its investigation. It can seek an emergency order for protection of an elderly person if that person needs protection but lacks mental capacity to accept or reject the services. It can also seek injunctions against any person who attempts to interfere with the providing of its services to an elderly person who has consented to the services.

The solution for my 66-year-old friend was a call to APS. They investigated, got her consent for providing assistance and took the legal action necessary to insulate her from threats and acts of violence.

If you witness questionable acts or know someone who may be abused, neglected or exploited, it is your duty to call Adult Protective Services.

Chapter 5: Wills

Why Have a Will?

Having a Last Will and Testament should be as common as having a checking account. You open a checking account because it is secure and convenient. You make a Last Will and Testament for the same reasons.

Why do thousands of people avoid making a Last Will and Testament? Here are three possibilities:

1. It makes you aware of your mortality, which makes many people feel uneasy;

2. It makes you deal with a lawyer, an experience many people would rather avoid; and

3. It costs money.

There are serious reasons to put these concerns aside and prepare a Last Will and Testament. Here are some reasons you should make a Last Will and Testament now:

- Intestacy: If you have no Last Will and Testament, Texas law determines who receives your assets when you die. If you are married with children, one-half of all you own goes to the children (not to your spouse).

- Failure to make a Last Will and Testament is equivalent to telling your spouse "When I die, you must make do with half of what we have now."

- Not having a Last Will and Testament does *not* mean you avoid probate. Lack of a Last Will and Testament often forces your survivors into the most complex probate procedure: Dependent Administration.

- A Last Will and Testament will simplify life for your survivors by:

  1. defining who gets your assets when you die;

  2. appointing someone to administer your affairs;

  3. selecting the least expensive and troublesome procedures; and

4.   listing alternative plans if your first plans cannot happen.

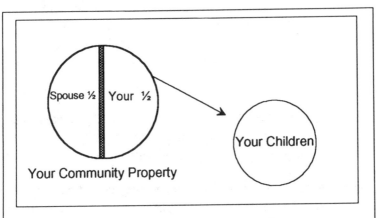

When you die without a Last Will and Testament, and have one or more children or grandchildren, your half of the Community Property passes to them. YOU HAVE CONDEMNED YOUR SURVIVING SPOUSE TO "GETTING BY" ON HALF OF THE COMBINED ASSETS.

◆   Not having a Last Will and Testament may cause higher estate taxes. The Estate Tax is our federal government's highest tax, topping out at 55%. There are many legal and ethical ways to reduce this burden, and to avail yourself of most of them, a Last Will and Testament is the first step.

◆   Not having a Last Will and Testament creates family quarrels. No matter how well your children get along, your death will cause anxiety and stress. Too often, this flares into disputes over family "treasures" or land. It separates brothers and sisters for decades. Your guidance at this stressful time, in the words of your Last Will and Testament, provides your family the direction it needs to stay together.

The effort it takes to prepare your Last Will and Testament today is inconsequential compared to the increased harmony it provides your family after you die.

Military: **Be cautious of wills prepared by the Judge Advocate's office on a military base. While these are often well done, they are just as often prepared poorly. Why? Frequently, the military attorney is not licensed to practice law in Texas. He therefore relies heavily on "forms" recommended by others in the office. The result can be a poorly drafted and inappropriate Will.**

Preparing a Last Will and Testament is not expensive or unsettling when you find the right attorney. Ask for a referral from your friends, your doctor or hospital, or your senior community center.

Dying Without a Will

If you have not acted to make a Last Will and Testament, you are "intestate." Texas law handles intestacy and your affairs like this (if you have a surviving spouse and children):

Dear spouse:

I leave all my half of our Community Property to the children. You will have to get by on your half of the assets we owned together, and they must be, in most instances, managed jointly by you and the children.

You may not sell any joint asset without all the children's consent. If they are adults, you have no control over their inheritance.

I give all of my Separate Property real estate to the children, none to you. I give 2/3 of my Separate Property personal assets (like mementos, heirlooms, and investments) to the children and 1/3 to you. You all can fight over which specific asset each gets.

If you and the children die before me, I give everything I own to my "heirs at law." No one knows who they are, so any relative may try for a piece of my estate.

I appoint you as my Administrator. However, your decisions will be subject to the control of a Judge and you must pay for insurance to cover any possible errors you make.

I require you to file a public inventory of all my assets. You must get the Judge's approval to sell or distribute any of my assets, or to invest and manage the assets. This must be done each time you desire to do anything in relation to my estate.

I am willing to pay a substantial portion of our assets in Estate or Inheritance taxes. I do not care to investigate methods for saving the money.

In conclusion, you and the children must start a confusing and expensive legal process. Instead of seeing my lawyer for a Last Will and Testament to make an easy transition after my death, I adopt state law as my 'Will'."

Signed: *Your Loving Spouse*

Without your own Last Will and Testament, these Texas laws of descent and distribution divide your assets. These laws require detailed and expensive legal procedures. Also, it is unlikely that they give your assets to the people you would have chosen.

On the other hand, pre-planning can streamline the procedure to save money and can identify your heirs and the items they are to receive. If you don't yet have a Last Will and Testament, you should make one.

Three Texas Will Varieties

Texas allows three varieties of the "Last Will and Testament," each with its own technicalities:

+ a spoken Will,

+ a handwritten Will, and

+ a formal Will.

Nuncupative (Spoken) Wills

Based on a statute dating to 1879, the days of trail drives and gunfights, the spoken Will was designed for frontier days when writing was not as common.

Many limitations are imposed on the spoken Will to increase its accuracy. Prized possessions (like a horse and saddle) should not be handled frivolously.

Hence, your spoken Will must be made during your last sickness while at home; if not at home, you must have been at another location for at least ten days before you can make a spoken Will, unless you are removed from your home due to sickness, then make the spoken Will, and die before you return home.

Clearly a cowpoke on a trail drive could not rely on a spoken Will to pass on his personal possessions. He wasn't at any particular location long enough to qualify.

Even if your location is correct, your spoken Will may give away no more than $30 worth of personal items unless three witnesses hear the Will spoken.

If six months passes between the date of speaking and the date of a Court hearing, the three witnesses must have written down what they heard spoken (but must have written it down within six days of hearing it spoken) for the spoken Will to be brought into court at all.

A spoken Will cannot be used to pass ownership to land under any circumstances. The writers of the law felt that land was too valuable a resource to be entrusted to the spoken word.

Finally, when it comes time to "probate" a spoken Will, the people who could have inherited if the spoken Will did not exist must be notified and have a chance to contest the spoken Will.

The question is: why go to all this trouble just to give away $30 worth of personal property? The spoken Will, while still found in the law books, has little use in today's society. You should have a correctly executed holographic or formal Will.

Holographic Wills

For a holographic Will to be valid, Texas law requires:

- ◆ it must be written entirely in your own handwriting,

- ◆ it must contain the date it was written, and

- ◆ it must be signed by you. Witnesses are not necessary.

Though handwritten wills are valid, they are not efficient and can cause problems. Since you prepare your own Will, you initially save some attorney's fees. But eventually the inefficiency of a handwritten Will overcomes the initial savings and the overall cost rises.

Three factors make a handwritten Will less reliable and potentially more expensive than a formal Will:

- ◆ If any part of the Will is not in your handwriting (for example, is typed or pre-printed) the Will is not valid. Avoid writing it on pre-printed letter-head or hotel stationery. Beware of "fill in the blank" Will forms that ask only for your signature at the end without witnesses; they will not be recognized as valid.

- ◆ Since you are writing your own Will you must be cautious about mistakes or incorrect use of words. The "plain meaning" of your words is not always the legal meaning that will be attached when your handwritten Will is interpreted by the court.

♦ Your handwritten Will is unlikely to contain legal "short-cuts" (that save time and money) which will be contained in formal wills written by professionals. Probate is likely to take much more time and be more expensive if courtroom probate is necessary.

With all of its difficulties, a handwritten Will is still better than no Will at all. If you do not currently have a Will, follow these easy steps:

1. take a blank sheet of paper,

2. in your own handwriting identify yourself, give the date, and describe where you want your assets to go when you die,

3. sign the handwritten Will, and

4. call your lawyer for an appointment to make a formal Will.

Formal Wills

The third type of Will, the "formal Will," is most thorough. Prepared by an attorney, it must be dated, signed by the person making the Will, and signed by two witnesses who are older than fourteen.

Your formal Will should take advantage of the following valuable options:

◆ Independent Administration. Using the correct legal wording in your will frees your Executor from detailed court supervision. This saves time and reduces attorneys fees.

◆ Waiver of Bond. Unless your Will states otherwise, Texas law requires your Executor to purchase a bond (an insurance policy guaranteeing the Executor will act honestly). The bond must be paid for from your assets. However, if you select an Executor you trust without reservation you can waive the bond and save the money.

◆ Self Proof. When you die and your Will goes before the Judge, reliable proof must be presented showing the document offered is indeed your Will.

There are three methods of proving a Will's validity:

The first requires the witnesses to testify in court. However, people in our mobile society tend to move frequently; they may be living in Arizona when you need them. Transportation costs and compensation add to your costs.

The second requires a handwriting expert (or two persons familiar with the signature of the Will's maker) to examine the Will if the witnesses are not available. They must appear before the Judge. The expert must be paid, which increases costs.

The third is best: a legal Self Proving Affidavit should be attached to your Will. You and the witnesses sign the affidavit after signing the Will, and the affidavit is notarized. After your death if the Will is presented to the Judge, the affidavit is complete proof. Because you pre-planned, an unnecessary cost was eliminated.

A formal Will should:

- Appoint an Executor, with alternate choices in case your first choice is not available, and

- Identify your heirs and alternate heirs if your first choices are not available.

A formal Will gives you the option of:

- Appointing guardians for your minor children;

- Creating a trust to protect your heirs; and

- Planning to reduce or eliminate estate taxes.

Military (and other new Texans) Question: **I recently moved to Texas after retirement. Do I need to make any changes to my Will?**

Answer:

Your old Will is probably "valid" in Texas, but your heirs may have a difficult time using it. Each state relies upon different legal formalities when probate time arrives.

Further, Texas is a Community Property state, so your Will may need adjustment for property you acquire after moving here.

At the least, your out-of-state Will should be modified (using a codicil) to include these Texas formalities:

- Appointment of an Independent Executor;
- a Self Proving Affidavit; and
- Waiver of the fidelity bond.

Question:

My mother's doctor just told her that she has cancer, with maybe six months to live. What do you think she should she do to prepare? Our father died four years ago.

Answer:

At this difficult time, your mother's emotional well-being is key. Without pushing her too fast, she should do the following:

Update her Will. Does it pass her property to those she chooses? Is the Executor (and any alternate) still her best selection? Was the will signed properly? A typed Will must have two or more witnesses, must be dated, and must be signed by her. It should also include a Self Proving Affidavit.

Look into establishing a "Living Trust" and placing the bulk of her assets into it. The Trustee can manage her finances without court supervision, and the assets pass without the need for probate. The trust can even continue after her death to provide for her children or grandchildren. (*See*, **Chapter on Living Trusts,** page 85).

Make a Power of Attorney for Asset Management. This allows an agent to pay bills, sell items to raise cash, and handle all her finances. If a "Living Trust" is used, the Power of Attorney covers anything omitted.

Sign a Power of Attorney for Health Care so someone close can make care decisions when she no longer can.

Consider a Natural Death Directive, if she wishes to stay off artificial life support machines.

Check her bank accounts to be sure someone has access. Consider making them "survivorship" accounts. Inventory the safe deposit box. Make a list of assets.

Review her life insurance and any pension. Are the Beneficiary choices in her policies up-to-date?

She may want to consider "hospice" care if her doctor concurs. Hospice is outpatient medical care which will focus on her comfort, not try to cure her.

Chapter 6: When is Probate Necessary?

What is Probate?

What is Probate? When is it necessary? What can be done to reduce the chances of needing probate?

Probate is the process of "proving" that a Will is valid. Although ownership of assets passes instantly to your heirs when you die, your Will is not usable as evidence of ownership unless probated.

A Will can be offered for probate only in the first four years after someone dies. After that, the courts will not accept an application for probate.

The goal of probate is to collect the estate's assets, pay debts and taxes, and distribute the remaining assets to the heirs.

Texas has several different types of probate, with different levels of complexity. The most common is "Independent Administration," where the Court has very little input. "Dependent Administration," on the other hand, relies on the Judge to approve almost all actions taken by the Executor (and is more expensive and time-consuming).

The need for probate depends primarily on these factors:

- The estate's complexity (not the size);

- The heirs' desire for clear and unquestionable title; and

- Efforts at avoiding probate by pre-planning.

What you own when you die (not how much) is a major factor. Assets that rely heavily on paperwork to show ownership -- like stocks & bonds, real estate, and bank accounts -- tend to force your estate into probate. Why? Because the people who process the paperwork are protected from certain risks if they deal with a duly appointed Executor.

Pre-Plan to Simplify

Pre-planning can make a tremendous difference. A proper Last Will and Testament is a basic necessity. Without a Will, estate administration may still be needed and is guaranteed to be more expensive and complex. With a proper Will, the cost and inconvenience of probate can be greatly reduced.

Other planning tools include a Community Property Survivorship Agreement, setting up other assets as "survivorship" property, using a funded Living Trust, and making gifts while you are living. Proper use of these tools might even eliminate the need for probate. These are each discussed in detail in other sections of this book.

Every situation is different. Talk to your attorney to decide what is best for you.

Chapter 7: Styles of Probate

First Steps

When a loved one dies, what legal steps must be taken?

Before you think about the legal ramifications, take stock of yourself. You have just suffered a very serious loss. During the first six months to a year after the loss, you should refrain from making big changes in your life. Don't sell the house yet. Act to enhance your security.

Don't wait too long before you start to get organized, though. Some people wait a few days, some wait years (which is too long and takes away many options). Ideally, you will feel ready to begin the legal process within four to eight weeks after the funeral.

Your first legal move should be to organize your paper-work. Locate these basic items:

- *1.* ◆ the original of the Last Will and Testament;

- *2.* ◆ the deed to the house and other real estate, and the mortgage papers if there is an outstanding loan;

- *3.* ◆ the certified death certificate;

- *4.* ◆ the car titles;

- *5.* ◆ the C.D.s, stocks, bonds, and other investments; and

- *6.* ◆ the social security number of your deceased family member.

Your second move should be to go to your family lawyer. If you don't have one, seek a referral from a reliable source like a close friend or your county bar association.

Military: **Some bases have a retirement service office. You will get a great deal of help from the highly trained volunteers there. They can assist you through the maze of military pension forms, burial allowances, and other benefits to which you may be entitled as a survivor.**

The Goals of Probate

The goals of probate are to collect the assets, pay debts and taxes, and distribute what is left to the heirs.

Probate is rarely the nightmare experience it is rumored to be. In fact, the term "probate" covers five basic legal procedures ranging from extremely complex to simple:

- Dependent Administration, the most complex procedure. It may be necessary when a person dies without having a Will, or when a person fails to simplify the process through instructions in his Will. In this method, the Executor must get prior court approval for most actions.

- Independent Administration, which is a simpler process than Dependent Administration. It is called "independent" because the Executor may act in most instances without prior court approval by following the instructions in the Will.

- Muniment of Title may be used when there are no debts to be paid. A court order acts as evidence that ownership has passed through the terms of the Will. In this procedure, no Executor is appointed.

- A Small Estate Affidavit may be filed if the estate is smaller than $50,000, has no debt and has no real estate. Again, no Executor is appointed. This does, however, require appearance before a judge..

◆ Finally, an "Affidavit of Heirship" might be filed with the county clerk. This process has the advantage of being inexpensive, and the disadvantage of being unreliable. No court approval is issued, and the affidavit does not have to be accepted as proof of title.

Dependent v. Independent Administration

The most complex probate, Dependent Administration, is supervised each step of the way by the probate court. Independent Administration is, on the other hand, free of the court's step-by-step oversight. Still, the first steps are identical in both.

To begin Dependent or Independent Administration, an attorney must be hired. He files a request asking the Judge to approve the Will (called "admitting the Will to probate").

Consider the probate process from the Judge's perspective: into court walks John Smith, whom the Judge has never met. John has a document which appears to be Betty Smith's Will. The Judge must ask: Is this really Betty's Will, or is it a fake? Is Betty really dead? Is my court the right place for these questions to be asked?

Proving the Will's Authenticity

The probate code provides a method for answering these questions. First, the authenticity of the Will must be established using one of these methods:

- The witnesses who saw Betty sign the Will can be located and brought to court. They can testify that the Will is really Betty's Will. However, witnesses cannot always be easily located because a Will might be 25 years old.

- If the actual witnesses cannot be located, anyone who knows Betty's handwriting well enough to identify her signature can be brought into court. They can testify that the Will appears to be Betty's. However, sometimes there are no such witnesses.

- If Betty had the foresight, her Will might be "self-proved." This is an affidavit attached to the Will and signed by Betty and her witnesses at the time they signed the Will. Under the probate code, a Self Proving Affidavit alone is adequate evidence for a judge to admit the Will to probate. This technique is the most reliable and least expensive.

Is Betty really dead? Someone (usually the Executor) must testify she is. He must also testify that Betty died in the County where this court sits, or that Betty had assets in that county. Otherwise, the Will is in the wrong forum.

Once satisfied, the Judge will order the Will admitted to probate.

Becoming an Executor

To appoint an Executor, the Judge must determine that the applicant is entitled to hold the position. Generally, the person named in the Will is "qualified" to be Executor. Only adults who are legally competent and have never been convicted of a felony may serve.

Before taking office, an Executor must post a bond unless the Last Will and Testament says that no bond is necessary. The bond is an insurance policy that guarantees honest action by the Executor.

Also, the Executor must take an oath of office in which he swears to fulfil the duties and responsibilities of the role.

Inventory of the Estate

Both Independent and Dependent Administration require filing of a public inventory of the assets of the estate within 90 days of the Executor's taking his oath of office. Also, a notice must be published in the newspaper telling any possible creditors where to send their claims.

Similarities End

The similarity between Dependent and Independent Administration stops at this point. It is here that an "Independent Executor" becomes independent: no further action is required of him in court.

The Dependent Executor, on the other hand, must continue to rely on the court for nearly every decision. If it is time to pay a debt of the estate, or to sell an asset of the estate, or to distribute property to the heirs, the Dependent Executor must first get approval from the Judge. Each time the Dependent Executor goes to court, he must:

- ◆ Hire an attorney (usually the same one who filed the probate originally);

- ◆ File with the court a motion requesting approval of the action he wants to take;

- ◆ Notify the public, through the Clerk's office, that he wants to take the action and that a public hearing will be held at the time chosen by the court;

- ◆ Appear in court at the proper time to present his request to the Judge. At this point, any person who objects to the action may present their opinion to the Court as well;

- ◆ Prepare an order for the Judge that approves the desired act (or which disapproves and for-

bids the act if the Court finds it to be need-
less).

If the court approves the desired action, the Dependent
Executor may then proceed to sell the asset or pay the
bill. When the action is finished, he must file a report informing the Court of the action taken and seeking "con-
firmation." And when the probate is finished, he must
file another inventory and ask the Judge for permission to
close the estate.

Muniment of Title

Probating a Last Will and Testament as a Muniment of
Title sounds intimidating. But use the word "evidence"
for "muniment" and the meaning becomes clear: the Will
is evidence of ownership.

Although simpler and less expensive than either Dependent or Independent Administration, the Muniment of
Title process is not available in all situations.

Probate as a Muniment of Title can only be used if the
estate owes no debts (other than, perhaps, a mortgage)
and if there aren't any other reasons for an Executor's
appointment. Business dealings like rental property, part-
nership, or being a creditor usually call for appointment
of an Executor.

For example, Harry dies owning a house (with a small
mortgage), other land, and a bank account. He does not

have any debt other than the mortgage. His estate probably qualifies for probate as a Muniment of Title. On the other hand, if he has several credit card debts he probably does not qualify.

An attorney is needed to probate a Will as a Muniment of Title. If you do not have an attorney, consult a reliable referral source.

The attorney prepares an "application" requesting a probate court hearing. The application is filed with the probate clerk and the sheriff gives notice to all interested persons by posting notice at the courthouse door.

About ten days later, the attorney and a person who was close to the deceased appear in court to testify that the Will is authentic. The Judge reviews the Will, the application and the proof. If the Judge is satisfied that all is in order, the Judge signs an order approving the Will.

The order approving the Will does several things: it establishes a legal fact that the Will is authentic, it instructs the clerk to record the Will in the county records, and it instructs anyone with assets belonging to the estate to turn them over to the heirs named in the Will without further legal complications. This allows the estate to be gathered and distributed to the heirs.

No Executor is appointed in a Muniment of Title proceeding. No oath is needed, no bond is posted, no inventory is prepared, and no court approval for future action is necessary. Within 181 days of the order's issuance a report should be made to the court detailing how the Will's instructions have been followed. After that, the probate is completed.

Small Estate Affidavit

In the case of a small estate, probate is not always necessary. A "Small Estate Affidavit" can be used if the estate owes no debt, owns no real estate, and is valued under $50,000. This is excellent when the decedent had modest savings, lived in a rented dwelling, and the survivors are cooperative and few.

A Small Estate Affidavit can be used in situations where a Will exists or when no Will exists. If there is a Will, the Will identifies the heirs by name. If no Will exists, then the state laws of descent and distribution determine who the heirs are.

Once identified, all of the heirs must join together to sign the affidavit. It must also be signed by at least two people who knew the deceased but who do not receive anything from the estate. All signatures must be notarized. The affidavit must be written by an attorney and filed with the probate court's small estate records. If you do not have an attorney, consult a reliable source for a referral.

A list of all of the heirs, including their names and addresses, must be included in the affidavit. A list of all the assets and debts of the deceased must be included.

After filing, the affidavit is assigned a case number. The heirs must wait at least thirty days after the date of death before filing the affidavit. However, since this is an abbreviated procedure, no notice of the filing need be given by the heirs or by the court.

Approval of the affidavit by the probate judge is mandatory, but no witnesses are needed and no testimony is taken. After approval, the affidavit is recorded in the clerk's records and the heirs get certified copies.

The affidavit and approving order identify which assets the heirs are entitled to receive and authorize banks, transfer agents, and other persons who hold assets of the estate to deliver those assets to the heirs. This procedure, however, cannot be used to transfer title to land. If land is involved, then probate of the Will as a "Muniment of Title" may be a more appropriate legal procedure.

Affidavit of Heirship

The final probate procedure is called "Affidavit of Heirship." It is the simplest and least expensive. It is also the least reliable since a probate judge never gives approval. The heirs will need an attorney to assist with preparation of the affidavit.

If the estate is mostly personal items or paid-for land, and if the entire family is agreeable (so there is little chance of a contest) then an Affidavit of Heirship might succeed.

The Affidavit of Heirship is a sworn statement about the life history of the deceased person. If a Will exists, it may be attached to the affidavit. The affidavit is signed by at least one person who knew the life history, is notarized, and then filed with the county clerk.

The filed affidavit is often, but not universally, accepted as evidence that title to the assets passed to the persons named in the affidavit. Once it has been on file for five years, the information in it is presumed to be true in any legal proceeding. If any parties want to contest the information, they can.

The heirs' preparation of an Affidavit of Heirship is not guaranteed to be the final act in an estate. Since it is not court approved, any interested person can impose a more complex procedure requiring court approval. If so, the affidavit is treated as non-binding evidence. This lack of guarantee is the Affidavit of Heirship's weakest point.

Chapter 8: Rights of Survivorship

Creating Rights

"Rights of Survivorship" are an easy way to give some-one ownership of an asset when you die. They are created either by agreement or by gift.

Usually, Rights of Survivorship are created by agreement. For example, a husband and wife can agree in writing that all of their community property will pass to the survivor between them when one of them dies. This is a "Community Property Survivorship Agreement," and must be filed with the county clerk.

Sometimes, survivorship rights can be "given" by the current owner. For example, a father can place his daughter's name onto his bank account and instruct that the bank pay all sums he has on deposit to his daughter when he dies. However, the agreement must be in writing, must be signed by father and daughter, and must specify that "Rights of Survivorship" are being granted.

Use With Caution

Survivorship rights must be used with caution. Why? Because they override your Last Will and Testament and may block your intentions.

Recently, some banks have begun to open ALL NEW ACCOUNTS automatically with Rights of Survivorship. They do this even when the parties have no knowledge of the effect of survivorship rights. This may cause more harm than good.

An example: *Elizabeth has three adult children. She intends for her assets to pass equally to all three children when she dies, and that is what her Last Will and Testament instructs.*

Her oldest son has been helping Elizabeth pay bills and she decides it is time to put his name on her checking account. When she changes her account at the bank, the bank's form creates "Right of Survivorship" for her son. Elizabeth is not told that she has created survivorship rights.

When Elizabeth dies, her checking account contains nearly 1/3 of her assets. Her son, as survivor, becomes the owner of that money regardless what the Last Will and Testament says. The result: her son gets the bank account and 1/3 of everything else under the Will. This is not an equal distribution!

What Elizabeth needed to do was coordinate more wisely her survivorship assets with her Last Will and Testament. When the bank routinely created survivorship rights without her consent, they altered her estate plan.

Working together, upon your death, your Last Will and Testament and Survivorship rights can pass your assets with ease. But working against each other, they can create chaos and family misery.

Your accounts should always harmonize with your Last Will and Testament. Check with your bank to see how you are set up.

Stauffer v. Henderson

Rights of Survivorship is an extremely useful technique for avoiding probate. It is also very cost effective. But it must be understood and used properly or it will not work for you.

A primary example of the failure to properly use Rights of Survivorship was announced by the Texas Supreme

Court on December 31, 1990, through its decision in *Stauffer v. Henderson.*

Here's what happened: Marion Henderson and Mary Stauffer were sisters. Marion Henderson opened a bank account. All money in the account came from Marion Henderson, who put her sister's name on the account as Joint Tenant (Marion "or" Mary). The account card read as follows:

> "Either of us shall have the power to act in all matters relating to such account, whether the other be living or dead, and that upon the death of either of us any balance in said account or any part thereof may be withdrawn by, or upon the order of the survivor. It is especially agreed that withdrawal of funds by the survivor shall be binding upon us and upon our heirs, next of kin...."

Marion Henderson died, and Mary Stauffer withdrew the money. J.D. Henderson, Marion's husband, sued to get the money back. He claimed that half the money was his because of Community Property laws and half belonged to Marion's estate.

Court's Ruling

The Texas Supreme Court ruled in favor of Mr. Henderson. The Court said that no Right of Survivorship was created by the account card even though it appeared to give the money to Mary Stauffer.

That decision is consistent, because years ago Texas law was structured to eliminate any "presumption" that Rights of Survivorship exist simply because two names are listed on an account. The only thing that can create binding Rights of Survivorship is a written agreement (like an account card). But you want to avoid the tremendous confusion over what wording to use to create survivorship rights.

In the Stauffer case, the Supreme Court decided that special language must be used. Just saying "joint property" was not enough. Instead, the agreement must explicitly say that the account is held as Joint Tenants WITH Rights of Survivorship. When used, that wording will create a valid survivorship agreement.

The Court says that Marion Henderson's account did no more than authorize withdrawal of funds by Mary Stauffer. The ability to withdraw the money, contrasted with the issue of "who owns the money" are two different things altogether.

If you intend to set up a joint account with Rights of Survivorship, be certain that the words "Joint Account with Rights of Survivorship" are written into the account agreement. Also be certain that both you and the intended survivor sign the account card. If done properly, Rights of Survivorship will assist you in avoiding probate.

Community Property Rights of Survivorship

In August 1989, spouses became able to use a "Community Property Survivorship Agreement" to automatically pass their community property to the survivor when one spouse dies. A properly written, signed, and filed agreement simplifies the complex tasks faced by a widow or widower. A Will is still necessary to cover issues which the survivorship agreement cannot address.

"Probate" of a Community Property Survivorship Agreement is not necessary. The agreement passes title to community property without any further action.

If a dispute arises, the probate court can guarantee validity of the agreement. The judge will need to see the original agreement, so keep it in a safe place and let someone else know where it is. Once an order is signed, anyone who should deliver property to the survivor may do so without hesitation.

Formalities

Both spouses must sign the agreement, which should be prepared by an attorney. You must then file it with the county clerk. The agreement is then ready to pass assets to the survivor without the need for extensive paperwork or court intervention.

Historically, our community property system, which we inherited from the Spanish, thwarted attempts by married couples to create "survivorship" arrangements for the couple's community property. When one of the spouses died, title could only pass to the survivor through the Last Will and Testament. The Community Property Survivorship Agreement changes that pattern.

A Will is still necessary for depth of planning. A Will is still the best way to:

- pass title to your separate property;

- name a "backup" heir if there is no surviving spouse; or

- pass assets to someone other than the surviving spouse.

The Community Property Survivorship Agreement is a planning tool you should strongly consider. When properly written it streamlines procedures, is straightforward and will save you time and money.

Military: **The legal offices at many military bases refuse to prepare Community Property Survivorship Agreements. Why? Perhaps they feel that this non-traditional approach to estate planning is too new to be tried.**

The opportunity to automatically pass your community property to your surviving spouse, without the need for complex probate procedures, is a new idea in Texas. But its legal foundation is very reliable. Our constitution was amended to allow the process, a statement that the voters desired the change. Our Probate Code was also amended to allow the procedure.

If you want to simplify your own estate, you should obtain, sign, and file a community property survivorship agreement.

Question:

My wife and I completed a Community Property Survivorship Agreement in January 1989, primarily to avoid probate. I recently heard that the August 1989 law changes have upset the apple cart by requiring these agreements to be probated. Is that correct? I heard that the 1987 constitutional amendment allowed community property survivorship rights, not the 1989 law. Is that correct?

Answer:

A Community Property Survivorship Agreement automatically passes title to a surviving spouse without further action. This means that no probate of the agreement is necessary. The statute states that: "An agreement between spouses creating a Right of Survivorship in Community Property that satisfies the requirements... is effective without an adjudication."

After the death of a spouse, the survivor can optionally apply to the court for an order stating that the agreement satisfies the requirements of law.

Your understanding that the 1987 constitutional amendment created the opportunity for community survivorship is accurate. The 1989 statute fills out the details of what the 1987 constitutional amendment made possible.

Question:

If you have a valid Will and a Community Property Survivorship Agreement, is it still necessary to probate the Will?

Answer:

Though the Agreement is intended to avoid probate there may still be reasons for probating your Will. Do you own separate property or want to give property to someone other than your surviving spouse? The survivorship agreement is limited to community property and is limited to passing title to your spouse only.

Question:

Is the Community Property Survivorship Agreement a form or a letter?

The agreement is a contract between you and your
spouse. No standard form has been printed commercially
for distribution. Contact your lawyer or Self Help Services for help (*See* the **Resources** chapter for information).

Question:

Can a Community Property Survivorship Agreement be
filed by being mailed to the County Clerk or must it be
hand carried?

Answer:

Either way. If mailing it, you may want to send it via certified mail to be sure it gets there. The clerk charges $3
for the first page being filed, and $2 for each added page
of the same document. The clerk will retain the original
for two to six weeks, then mail it back to you.

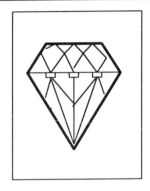

Chapter 9: Partition of the Community Estate

Community Property

When a married couple has different opinions on disposition of their properties, what can be done? Community property can equitably be converted into separate property.

In Texas, all property acquired during marriage is community property. The only exceptions are the things you owned before marriage, or items you received during marriage as a gift, inheritance or by partition between you and your spouse. These things are separate property.

Community Property	Separate Property
Acquired during marriage including: - Earnings - Interest - Appreciation - Dividends	Acquired before marriage begins or after marriage ends, plus: - Gifts received - Inheritances received - Items partitioned from the Community estate

Partition

The Texas Family Code allows you and your spouse, in a written partition agreement signed by both of you, to convert some or all of your community property into separate property. You may record the agreement with your county clerk, a practice I strongly encourage.

The partition may be done by the two of you at any time during your marriage. It can include property that is currently community and property that might become community in the future.

It can contain terms which allow the income from your separate property to remain separate property. Since all acquisitions during marriage are community property, any interest earned (even on a separate property bank account) is community property, unless the agreement says that earnings from separate property are to retain their separate property identity. The agreement is the only way to override the creeping commingling of assets that may result.

Fraud Not Allowed

The partition is not valid if it is done to "defraud" a pre-existing creditor of one of the spouses. Also, one of the spouses may later challenge the validity of the agreement by proving that:

- the agreement was not signed voluntarily, or

- the agreement was "unconscionable" when it was signed, and that before signing, the challenger did not know and was not provided with a fair and reasonable disclosure of the assets and debts of the other spouse.

You should hire an attorney to draw up the agreement and to review your wills to be sure they conform to your new pattern of ownership.

Chapter 10: Bank Accounts & Safe Deposits

'And' v. 'Or'

When setting up your bank accounts, two little words, "AND" and "OR," are important. If two names go onto a bank account, you need to pick between "AND" and "OR" to join them. What happens when you choose, and why is it important?

The word "AND" binds the two listed people together as a single unit. If the account lists "Herschel AND Bernice," the bank must deal with both of them. The word "OR" gives the bank a choice between the two people. If the account lists "Herschel OR Bernice," the bank can deal with either one of them.

If a bank account reads "Herschel AND Bernice," then the bank will require both of their signatures to access the account. If one of the owners dies, many banks will lock the account until they receive legal evidence on who is entitled to the account.

An example: you become ill and need someone to pay your bills. Your bank account lists two names joined with "AND." The second person cannot pay your bills because your signature is required for access. Guardianship may result.

If your bank account lists two names joined with "OR," then the second person can pay the bills. Only one signature is required for access. Making a Power of Attorney, before the need arises, is another way for you to plan for your care.

Choose carefully when you put another person's name on your bank account. Setting up an "OR" account gives unrestricted access to the account. If your assistant is unethical, you may lose your money. An "AND" account exists to act as a control over the account by requiring double signatures.

Who is the Owner?

Who owns the money in the account? Regardless of whether you choose the word "AND" or the word "OR," while both parties are alive the owner of the money is the person who owned the money before it was deposited. If you put $5,000 from your pocket into the bank, and ask your child to be the "OR" signature, and then you die, your estate owns the money -- not your child.

If your want your child to become the owner of the account when you die, you have two choices:

- ♦ say it in your Will, or

- ♦ ask your bank to set up the account "with Rights of Survivorship" (ROS). A ROS account can be either an "AND" or an "OR" account. When the funds owner dies, the other signer becomes the owner without any further proceedings. (*See, Stauffer v. Henderson* section, page 61 for more details).

Safe Deposit Box Rules

If you have a safe deposit box at the bank, what papers should you put in it? Can your Last Will and Testament and life insurance policies go there? Won't the bank seal the box when you die?

Prior to 1989, Texas law said when you die your safe deposit box is sealed until a properly appointed representative opens it. This law caused many people to avoid storing important papers in their safe deposit box.

But under a 1989 amendment to the Texas banking laws, if you and another person have a joint safe deposit box and one of you dies, the Bank must give the survivor access to the box and must allow any items to be removed from the box.

For example: Rhonda and Sam (who are married) have a safe deposit agreement with the bank which says they are "Joint Tenants." Under the former law, when Sam died Rhonda was locked out of the box. Under the new law, Rhonda has the right to open and empty the box without any controls.

If you have a safe deposit box in your name only, who can get in? The bank may permit an examination of the box, with no court order, by any of the following people: your surviving spouse, your parents, any of your adult descendants, or an possible Executor who presents a document that looks like a copy of your Last Will and Testament.

Under the above conditions, the box would be examined in the presence of a bank officer. Legally, the bank is allowed to deliver specific items to certain people only:

- ◆ your Will -- but it can only be given to the Probate Clerk;

- ◆ your life insurance policies -- they can be given only to the policy beneficiaries; and

- ◆ the deed to a burial plot -- it can be given to the person who is examining the box.

- No other items can be removed from the box until court authority is obtained.

Always store important papers in a secure yet accessible place. A safe deposit box can be a smart choice. Your survivors may be able to get into your safe deposit box with minimal effort, depending on the pre-arrangements you have made with the bank.

Chapter 11: Powers of Attorney

Durable Power of Attorney

Regular v. Durable

The two basic types of Power of Attorney are Durable and Regular.

A Regular Power of Attorney becomes invalid if you become disabled in any way. A Durable Power of Attorney, however, stays in force even if you are unconscious. Durable powers of attorney continue to work until the moment of your death unless you revoke them.

To be Durable, your Power of Attorney must contain specific legal language indicating that the powers you are granting will not terminate if you become disabled.

A Durable Power of Attorney can save time and money and can reduce confusion if you become unable to handle your own finances. You need not be wealthy to find uses for a Durable Power of Attorney.

Grant of Power

By signing a Durable Power of Attorney, you give someone of your choice (an Agent) power to act in your place.

You can grant unlimited powers to your agent, or you can grant very narrow powers. You can be as specific as you want. For estate planning, the powers granted are usually extensive to allow your agent flexibility.

Caution must be used when appointing an agent. If the powers are broad, your agent might dishonestly use your assets for your agent's gain. You must always take extra care to select an agent who is trustworthy.

If you are nervous about the lack of supervision inherent in a Power of Attorney, you might consider a Living Trust. More complex and expensive yet more comprehensive solutions, living trusts are also private and can help you avoid probate. They allow a Trustee, who you choose, to manage your finances when you become unable. A Trustee has well defined responsibilities and limitations.

Texas requires a Durable Power of Attorney to be made in writing, signed by you, witnessed by two adults, and filed with your county clerk.

Your Agent's powers exist until they expire (if the document contains a termination date) or until they are revoked by you. Revocation must also be in writing, signed, and filed with the county clerk.

While you should be cautious in choosing your agent and you must follow state-mandated procedures, a Durable Power of Attorney streamlines legal procedures and cuts costs, keeps your private business confidential, and helps you avoid Guardianship.

1989 Law Change

Question:

I understand durable powers of attorney must be witnessed. I have a Power of Attorney written in 1986 that is not witnessed. Is it still valid?

Answer:

The 1989 law change accepted old unwitnessed powers of attorney as still valid. Even so, there are three reasons you should replace your 1986 document.

> 1. Older powers of attorney become "stale."
>   Your agent's power is often refused by banks

and others who prefer to err on the side of caution. They want proof that the Power of Attorney has not been revoked, and you frequently cannot provide satisfactory evidence.

2. The 1989 law requires new durable powers of attorney to be filed with the county clerk. The only way to revoke one is by filing a revocation with the county clerk. When the bank searches the county records and finds the new Power of Attorney, but does not find a revocation it is "proved" that the new Power of Attorney is still valid.

3. The 1989 law requires acceptance of a properly written "new" Durable Power of Attorney by the third party to whom it is presented. If a new Power of Attorney says: "I authorize my agent to indemnify and hold harmless any third party who accepts and acts under this Power of Attorney," then the third party has to accept it.

Updating to a new Power of Attorney assures that when action is needed, the Power of Attorney will be accepted. Even though your 1986 Power of Attorney is legal, it can be refused. To be on the safe side, you should update according to the new law.

Your Aging Parent

Question:

My mother is in a nursing home, but her mind is very sharp. The nursing home tells me I need to set up Guardianship for my mother in case she takes a turn for the worse. What are my options?

Answer:

Guardianship cannot be started unless your mother has already lost mental capacity. Since her condition is good, the better option for both of you is a Power of Attorney.

Guardianship should be avoided if possible. It is Court supervised and your freedom to assist your mother is tightly controlled. Her mental status must decline before you can initiate Guardianship, when it must be proved that your mother is mentally incompetent or unable to handle her day-to-day personal affairs.

On the other hand, powers of attorney offer privacy, flexibility and convenience. You will need two different kinds of Power of Attorney: Durable Power of Attorney for asset management; Durable Power of Attorney for Health Care.

With a Durable Power of Attorney for asset management, she can give you power to assist with her finances. Be sure it is a "durable" Power of Attorney with special wording to keep it from expiring upon her disability. If it does not have the special wording, it becomes invalid when your mother becomes incompetent (just when you need it most).

A Durable Power of Attorney must be made in writing, signed by your mother, witnessed by two adults, and filed with the county clerk. It lasts until it expires, or until your mother revokes it or dies.

With a Durable Power of Attorney for Health Care, your mother can give you power to make health care decisions for her if she later becomes incompetent.

This must be written in a special format, and must be signed in the presence of two qualified witnesses. Before signing, your mother must read and sign a disclosure form.

Any decision you make must be based on what your mother would have wanted. Control, ultimately, remains with your mother: she may veto any medical decision you make.

When using the Power of Attorney for Health Care, you are not personally liable to pay for your mother's care unless you separately agree to. Without it, payment might be due from you directly if your mother cannot pay.

Chapter 12: Living Trusts

Goals of a Living Trust

There are several kinds of Trusts. Most you set up to benefit someone you love after you die. The exception is a Living Trust, which you set up to solve your own estate and probate problems. It may also help you achieve other commendable goals while you are living and able to see the benefits.

A Living Trust allows a manager (Trustee) to control your assets for you after you transfer ownership to the trust. It is called "living" because it is designed to assist you during your lifetime.

Why would you want to set up a Living Trust? Here are four common goals:

1. To help you avoid probate;

2. To help you provide continued care for yourself;

3. To help you protect your assets; and

4. To assist your loved ones.

Avoiding Probate with a Living Trust

One requirement of a Living Trust is that you transfer ownership of your assets to the trust. Why? A trust cannot die, so when the trust owns the assets there can never be probate of those assets.

Probate may still be needed if you leave assets outside the trust (perhaps you acquired them after it was set-up). A Will is still needed to dispose of the incidental personal items you possess.

Funded v. Unfunded Trusts

Assets can be transferred two ways:

- ♦ you can change title to your assets the same time the trust is established (a "funded" trust), or

- ♦ you can put in only enough to start the trust's existence (an "unfunded" trust).

An unfunded trust is more complex: since the goal is to have the trust own your assets at the time of your death, a strategy must be devised to achieve that goal. This is usually done with a Durable Power of Attorney.

Here's how it works: You set up an unfunded trust -- putting perhaps $100 into a new bank account under the trust's name. At the same time, you create a Durable Power of Attorney, authorizing your agent to "dump" your estate into the trust if you become ill. The agent must be relied upon to follow your instructions, and must act quickly since his powers cease when you die.

Using a funded trust is a more certain strategy. With it, you create the trust and see that your assets are transferred at that time. There is no reliance on an agent, nor is there a risk that your death will be too sudden for your agent to respond and "dump" assets into the Living Trust.

Military Tip: **Using a Funded Living Trust is a particularly effective way to avoid the confusion that results when you own real estate in more than one state. Typically, if you reside in Texas yet own land in another state, you must probate your Will in both places. Removing the asset from your testamentary estate (that is, allowing it to pass to your heirs through the terms of the trust instead of your Will) you can avoid probate twice.**

Protecting You and Your Assets

When you establish a Living Trust, you are typically the Beneficiary and the Trustee. Why would you want to transfer ownership of your assets into trust and let someone else manage them?

The answers are many: you may be overly "challenged" by management of the property, and want assistance. Perhaps your spouse has died, leaving you alone and in charge for the first time. You may have been informed of an illness, and want to plan an orderly transition. Or maybe you are retiring and plan to travel a good part of the year, and you need someone at home to guard the nest-egg.

Setting up the Living Trust includes planning for your own care. As the Beneficiary, you should be entitled to all of the income generated by the trust, and should be entitled to withdraw assets from the trust.

When you become ill or incapacitated, the trust management is not interrupted. The Trustee (a person selected by you) continues to handle your business affairs as a fully capable manager. Investments continue without interruption, payments are made on time, and your expenses are managed.

When you become ill, your designated Trustee would be required to pay all medical bills and provide for your continuing health care.

Providing for Your Loved Ones

Assisting your loved ones with a Living Trust offers considerable flexibility. You can choose your approach: providing assistance while you are alive, continuing care of your estate after your death, or both.

For example: James and Martha have been married 48 years. James has always handled the family finances, but he hasn't been doing so well lately. The doctor fears Alzheimer's disease may be slowly disabling James.

James and Martha decide to set up a Living Trust and to transfer their home, C.D.s, stock, savings, and cars to the trust. They select their oldest daughter to act as Trustee. Their goal: to be sure that James's illness does not reduce their income or ruin their reputations. Additionally, they want Martha to be cared for as long as she lives, and their grandson's college education to be encouraged.

The Living Trust for James and Martha will put their daughter in charge. She can invest the assets conservatively to protect the principal and generate income. She will then apply the income to pay James's medical bills and Martha's living expenses.

As James becomes less capable, there is no freeze on assets. Daughter continues management without interruption. If James were still in charge, bills would be left unpaid, investments would be left unattended. Martha would be in real trouble, especially if James's signature were required on something. She might be unable to access their savings, and be forced to start Guardianship proceedings. But the Living Trust has made these difficulties vanish.

After several years, James dies. There is no probate since he did not own anything. The trust continues for Martha's benefit. Martha's period of mourning and depression has no effect on the finances, since Daughter is still managing all funds.

When Martha dies, there is also no probate since she doesn't own any assets. The trust continues in Daughter's capable hands, providing a college fund for their grandson. When he is out of college, Daughter is permitted to terminate the trust and distribute the remaining funds as instructed in the Trust years earlier by her parents.

James and Martha's foresight in setting up the trust helped them avoid ruin during James's illness, provided for Martha's continued security, helped pay for college for grandson, and ultimately released the funds to their heirs. All without a moment in court, and all as a private and confidential transaction.

Choosing the Trustee

Selecting the proper Trustee is the key to a successful Living Trust. Your Trustee is the manager of the trust assets, and is the person who must follow the instructions laid out in the trust.

With a Living Trust, you may be your own primary Trustee. What is the benefit? As your own primary Trustee, there is little practical difference between before and after the trust was established. Legally, though, you no longer own the assets; the trust is owner.

So long as you are healthy, you can continue to be your own Trustee. But when you become ill, or simply desire management assistance, the Trust instrument will provide for an alternate Trustee to assume your duties. The transition is "seamless" --- there is no need for court intervention or legal process to hand over control.

You can also elect to turn over control from the beginning. If you do, you must select several persons to serve as Trustee in sequence. The goal is always to have a Trustee you have chosen, and never be left to rely on the courts to appoint a Trustee for you.

Selecting your Trustee and alternates must be done carefully. Choose someone you trust deeply, who has good business sense, and who desires to assist you. The emotional component should not be overlooked: your Trustee becomes your caretaker and watchdog. For this important role, you should select someone with whom you will be comfortable.

Your Trustee has very specific legal rights and duties spelled out in the Texas Trust Act. These provisions can be adjusted in the Living Trust agreement to fit your desires.

Your Living Trust provides unique planning alternatives. If the goals we've discussed match your goals, you should consider a Living Trust.

Question:

What is the difference between a "Living Trust" or "loving trust"?

Answer

The "Living Trust" and "loving trust" are the same thing. "Loving trust" is a trademarked name used for marketing purposes. The people who sell "loving trusts" conduct seminars with attorneys and financial planners. Their aim is to sell you a trust. Take their advice as only part of your decision-making process.

Pros and Cons

Living trusts are a useful tool, but you should investigate all your alternatives. Is the Living Trust the right tool for you?

A Living Trust is designed to achieve some very specific estate planning goals. "Pros" are:

- A Living Trust will assist in the management of your assets if you become ill;

- A Living Trust will provide monetary benefits to you and your loved ones; and

- A Living Trust may simplify or eliminate probate after your death.

Other aspects of a Living Trust depend on your attitude. There are several complicating factors when a Living Trust is established -- some people may find them to be drawbacks, some may find them beneficial:

- A Living Trust requires you to transfer ownership of your assets out of your name. Ownership of assets must be registered with the trust itself, (perhaps making you feel that you are losing control of your assets). However, you are allowed to be the Trustee of your own Living Trust (which means that so long as you are competent, you are the manager of the trust).

- A Living Trust must be dealt with regularly for the rest of your life. It is the active owner of your resources, and you are its Beneficiary. When you want money, you must deal with the trust. When you sell an asset you must deal with the trust. When you receive income, you must deal with the trust. Many feel that this is no burden, but some people never get comfortable with the new style of asset management.

- A Living Trust can eliminate probate in the estate of each "grantor" (creator of the trust). To do so, ALL OF YOUR ASSETS must be owed by the trust. If you leave a single stock certificate, a single bank account, or a single plot of land outside the trust, probate may still be necessary.

These three goals can be fulfilled with a Living Trust. They can also be met by using a combination of other planning techniques, including POWERS OF ATTORNEY, JOINT OWNERSHIP WITH RIGHTS OF SURVIVORSHIP, and, of course, with a WILL.

Don't ever jump to conclusions as to what is right for you. See a trained legal advisor to compare and contrast the costs and benefits of a Living Trust versus other planning techniques. Always aim to achieve your goals with as simple and cost effective an approach as possible.

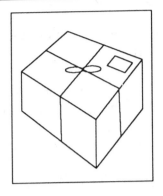

Chapter 13: Gifts and Charitable Giving

Gifts to Family Members

Any time you wish, you may give away all or any part of what you own. Frequently, gifts are given to children or grandchildren. Although no special reason is needed, you might give one of your children extra money to pay back a loan or you might give a grandchild money for college tuition.

But whenever you make a gift, you must think about federal gift tax. Gift taxes and Estate taxes are very similar (as a matter of fact, the gift tax and estate tax rates and deductions were "unified" in 1982).

Follow these basic rules when you make non-charitable gifts:

You have an annual IRS gift tax "exclusion" of $10,000. This means you may give any person up to $10,000 in any year without even thinking about the gift tax effect. The exclusion covers an unlimited number of recipients.

Here's an example: You have three children and six grandchildren. You may give each of them $10,000 (for a total of $90,000) without worrying about gift taxes. You can do this one time every year if you want.

Your annual exclusion can be combined with your spouse's exclusion to double the amount you can give away in a year without gift tax. This is called "split-giving."

In the above example, you and your spouse together would be able to give each recipient $20,000, for a total of $180,000. However, you must file a gift tax return to claim the benefit of a split gift. No tax will be due.

If you give an individual more than $10,000 in a year, you must file a gift tax return. This does not mean that you will have to pay gift taxes, because the tax may be offset by your Unified Credit against gift and estate tax. The Unified Credit is discussed more fully in the Estate Tax chapter, page 151.

Charitable Giving

Most people know the Internal Revenue Code is not designed only to collect government revenues; it is also a primary vehicle for social reform. Allowing you to reduce your taxes by sending money to a charity encourages and motivates charitable behavior. No gift tax is charged when you make a donation to charity.

Income Tax Effect

In their most basic form, charitable gifts are quite simple. For example, you give $1000 to the Arthritis Foundation, you take a $1000 deduction from your income tax. In the 28% bracket, you eliminate $280 of income tax that year.

Charitable deductions from your income tax cannot be more than one-half of your "adjusted gross income" -- that is, your income after deducting IRA, Keogh, or SEP contributions. If, for example, you had $80,000 income and made a $7,000 Keogh contribution, your "adjusted gross income" is $73,000. Half of that, or $36,500, is your maximum allowable charitable income tax deduction for that year.

Estate Tax Effect

You can reduce the size of your estate through an irrevocable charitable gift. For example, if you give $30,000 to charity, the following happens:

You save $8,400 on that year's income tax if you are in the 28% bracket. You reduce the size of your estate by $30,000, and after your death pay less estate tax. Tax savings depend on the overall size of your estate; the most you will save is 55%, so a $30,000 reduction in your estate reduces taxes by $16,500. Because of income tax and estate tax savings, your $30,000 gift actually costs you only $5,100.

Ways to Give

There are various ways to donate to a charitable organization:

- Give cash, which makes evaluating your gift very easy.

- Give personal property or real estate. The value of this type of gift is more difficult to define, and you may have to pay for an appraisal to substantiate your tax deduction.

- Give life insurance, which multiplies the power of your dollar. If you give a charity $30,000, that is the whole amount they receive. But if you buy life insurance, using the $30,000 to pay a single premium, the charity will receive the entire death benefit which should greatly exceed $30,000.

- Give your charity upon your death a more loosely defined benefit, like the income or the "left-overs" (remainder) from an investment.

This can be accomplished by using more complex methods: charitable trusts or pooled income funds.

More Complex Charitable Gifts

Because it may be unsettling to you to give away enough of your asset base to significantly reduce your taxes, more complex methods of "giving" have been devised so you can retain certain benefits at the same time you are helping a charity. Here are some examples:

The Pooled Income Fund

When you make a gift to a charitable organization under this method, the organization pools gifts from a variety of donors and you receive interest payments on your donation for your lifetime. However, income paid to you by the fund is taxable just like any other.

In the year you make the pooled income fund contribution, you get an income tax deduction for the value of the "remainder" (calculated using IRS provided figures). For example, if you are 62 years old and give a Pooled Income Fund $25,000 with guaranteed interest of 5%, the value of the remainder and your deduction is $12,007. In the 28% bracket, this results in a tax savings of $3,362 the first year.

After your death, the charity keeps the principal of the gift. Your estate gets the added benefit of being smaller and therefore paying less tax. In the 50% estate tax bracket, this amounts to saving another $12,500. Overall, your tax savings are $15,862 and you were paid interest on the full $25,000!

Your gift to a Pooled Income Fund must be irrevocable. The charitable institution pays to have the Fund's legal charter created, so the gift should not have any extra legal fees. Many other donors make contributions to the same Fund, and all the contributions are pooled.

The Charitable Remainder Trust

This is similar to a Pooled Income Fund, but is not pooled with other donor's gifts. You make a gift to charity and receive income for life. You pay income tax on any income you receive. You may structure your trust income to be guaranteed or to fluctuate.

You benefit by receiving a tax deduction when you make the gift, by keeping income, and by reducing the size of your estate.

Two Varieties

If your income fluctuates, it is because you chose to base your return on a percentage of the trust's fluctuating annual value. This is called a **Unitrust**. If your income is fixed, it is because you chose to calculate your return as a fixed portion of the value of the gift. This is called an Annuity Trust.

Variation 1: The Unitrust

For example, if you make a gift of $25,000 to a Unitrust promising to pay 5%, your income will vary. In the first year, the trust might purchase stock and bonds valued at $25,000. Your 5% income would be $1,250. In the second year, the stock market might go up so the trust assets are now worth $27,000. Your 5% income would be $1,350 the second year.

Variation 2: The Annuity Trust

If you give $25,000 to an Annuity Trust required to pay 5% interest, your income will be constant. Each year, regardless of the value of the trust or the amount of its income, it would pay you $1,250.

For either type of Charitable Remainder Trust, you may deduct from this year's income tax the value of the remainder to be kept by the charity. However, the deduction amount differs for an Annuity Trust and a Unitrust because the amount left over for the charity varies for each type.

The Annuity Trust tax deduction is the value of your gift minus the value of your annuity. If you are 62 and give $25,000 while keeping a 5% return, the IRS values your deduction at $16,000. In the 28% bracket, this would reduce your income tax the first year by $4,480.

The Unitrust tax deduction is the value of the remainder, calculated using IRS provided figures. If you are 62 and give $25,000 while keeping a 5% variable return for life, the deduction is valued at $11,620. In the 28% bracket, that reduces your income tax by $3,254 this year.

The Charitable Lead Trust

This is the exact opposite of remainder trusts and pooled income funds. In lead trusts, you make a gift to charity and the charity gets to keep the income instead of you. However, when the trust ends, the original gift amount is returned to you or your heirs.

You benefit by getting an income tax deduction each year the trust is in effect. You also get the pleasure of assisting a worthy charity while retaining your estate for your heirs.

The amount paid to the charity may be a guaranteed annuity or a unitrust amount. The annuity is a fixed payment chosen by the donor for a certain number of years or for the whole lifetime of the donor. The unitrust amount is a set percentage of the original donation paid to the charity for a certain number of years or for the whole life of the donor.

For example, you create a Charitable Lead Annuity Trust. You fund the trust with $50,000 and require that the income of $5,000 be paid to the charity each year.

Each year you would be entitled to deduct from your income tax the $5,000. In the 28% bracket, that is an annual savings of $1,400.

When you die, the trust could cease its payments to the charity and then the $50,000 can pass to your heirs. Your estate tax is not reduced with this technique. The wise managers of the charity could have used some of your annual contribution to buy life insurance payable to the charity when you die. If so, the death benefit would go tax free to the charity.

Chapter 14: Guardianship

Declarations of Guardian

While you are still healthy, you may decide to choose someone to become your Guardian should you need one some time in the future. This decision made in good faith and after careful consideration, gives you complete control over your own future Guardianship. (*See* **Appendix B** for a sample).

A "Declaration of Guardian" may be made by a competent adult. It must be written, signed, and witnessed by two people. The person chosen as Guardian cannot witness. The Declaration must be notarized.

You may also "disqualify" any person from ever being your Guardian under any circumstances. This protects you from people you may want to avoid, such as former spouses. If you name your spouse as Guardian but later are divorced, he or she is automatically disqualified.

The Declaration must have a "Self Proving Affidavit" to allow a Judge to accept your choices. This affidavit is proof you were competent at the time you signed the Declaration and that the Guardian will act in your "best interest."

You do not need to file this declaration with the court in advance; however, the person you chose as Guardian will need to file it when he or she goes to court to become your Guardian (if the need arises for one). Keep the original in a safe place, and let your intended Guardian know about it.

Your Declaration should list a first choice for Guardian and several back-ups. If the first choice is not available when needed, the alternates will be in line to replace the first choice.

A Declaration of Guardian may be revoked by tearing it up, or by making a new declaration that supersedes the old one.

'Plenary' or Full Guardianship

If someone you love can no longer handle his finances or take care of his physical needs, and he has not made a

Durable Power of Attorney, court controlled Guardianship becomes a real possibility.

Guardianship Strips Rights

By law, when a Guardian is appointed to supervise another person, the Ward is stripped of the right to make a binding contract, the right to vote, the privilege of driving, the right to get married, and the right to buy or sell real property. All decisions are made by the Guardian.

The Guardian needs Court approval before spending money or selling assets, even for the Ward's benefit. A lawyer must be hired. A request for approval of the desired action must be filed. Notice must be given. A public hearing must be held.

The Court will favor appointing your spouse as Guardian. If your spouse is unavailable, any "next of kin" can be next in line. Any person not "disqualified" can be Guardian (whether or not that person is related to the Ward).

A potential Guardian is disqualified if he:

- is under age 18,
- has "notoriously bad" conduct,
- is incompetent,

♦ is a party (or his parent is a party) to a lawsuit on which the welfare of the proposed Ward may depend,

♦ owes money to the Ward or has a claim against the Ward, or

♦ cannot prudently assist the Ward.

Filing Application

To begin a Guardianship, an interested person hires an attorney to prepare an Application for Guardianship, which is filed with the Court Clerk.

If the proposed Ward is 60 or older, his spouse, siblings, and all children must be mailed notice before a court hearing can take place. This requirement that the family be notified is fairly new, and will help avoid the need for unnecessary guardianships.

At the court hearing, it must be proved the Ward is of unsound mind, that the applicant is not "disqualified," and that the Ward's rights will be protected by appointment of a Guardian. If the Judge determines these facts exist, she will authorize the Guardianship by signing an order appointing the Guardian, which becomes effective when Letters of Guardianship are issued by the court's clerk.

Before Letters of Guardianship are issued by the clerk, the Guardian must post a bond and file an oath that he will act properly. Then an inventory of the ward's assets must be filed, reviewed, approved, and updated annually.

How to Avoid Guardianship

To avoid Guardianship, before losing mental capacity, you can take advantage of the laws by:

- ◆ signing a Durable Power of Attorney, and

- ◆ signing a Durable Power of Attorney for Health Care.

These private steps are easier, assure privacy, and virtually eliminate the need for complicated and expensive Guardianship proceedings.

Limited Guardianship

In certain instances, "full" Guardianship is just too extreme a solution to be used properly. For example: two months ago, Mrs. Right's husband was incapacitated after a mild stroke. He has not made powers of attorney. He is too ill to take care of business matters, but he can still make some decisions for himself.

Since Mr. Right did not make any powers of attorney, Guardianship may be the only way to continue doing business. But he can still take care of some things himself, so "full" Guardianship, which would strip him of all rights, is too extreme.

Limited Guardianship, a less extreme option, is more favorable to the Ward. Texas law requires that limited Guardianship "encourage the development of maximum self reliance and independence of the individual."

Limited Guardianship was first available only for the mentally retarded, but in 1983 the law made limited Guardianship available for any "incapacitated person." The incapacities must be displayed no more than six months before the start of Guardianship, and cannot be isolated events of bad judgment.

The Limited Guardian may only provide assistance in the areas where the Ward cannot himself function due to mental or physical disabilities. A limited Ward retains all civil rights, is presumed competent, and retains all rights not removed by court order.

To initiate Limited Guardianship, an attorney must file a petition asking the Court to act. Notice must go out to all appropriate family members. A Court hearing must be held, and the proposed Ward must be present unless the judge says otherwise. The proposed Ward is entitled to a lawyer.

When limited Guardianship is allowed, the Guardian gets only those powers specifically granted by the judge and no others. The Ward retains all other rights. Because of this, limited Guardianship demands a very detailed decision by the judge.

Although Limited Guardianship is legal and proper, you will find many lawyers and judges do not use it. Why? Perhaps because it is a much more detail oriented process. It takes a great deal more time to establish a useful Limited Guardianship than it does to grant plenary Guardianship. Still, if you feel Limited Guardianship is the best option in your circumstances, it is available.

Chapter 15: Long-Term Care

Financial Risks

One of the greatest financial risks faced by Senior Texans is the prospect of long-term care in a nursing facility.

Paying for this care takes careful planning, which can only be done if you understand your options and their limitations. This chapter will discuss private and government funding of long-term care.

There are three ways to pay for nursing home care. First, out of your own pocket or your family's pocket. Second, through insurance. Finally, through a government program.

Who Pays What?

Do not rely on Medicare to pay for your long-term care. In 1987, of nearly $41 billion spent on long-term care, Medicare paid only 1.4%. Medicaid paid 43.9%; the patients or their families paid 49.3%. About 1% was paid by private insurance and the rest by a variety of other sources.

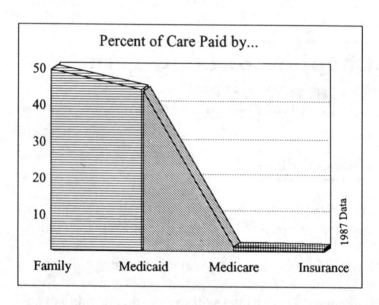

Medicare coverage for long-term care is very limited. At most, it will pay for a short nursing home stay after hospitalization. And Medicaid is simply not available to most elderly persons.

As they exist today, don't look to government programs as your solution to funding long-term care costs.

Military: **The VA provides some long-term care. Problem: long waiting lists. Several VA Hospitals have "Extended Care and Therapy Centers." These are like nursing facilities, but their goal is to rehabilitate patients and return them to the community. Not all patients will be accepted for care. Contact your local VA office for information.**

Nursing Home Insurance

Long-term Care (LTC) insurance has become a major concern since the Medicare Catastrophic Coverage Act was repealed.

LTC insurance may help avoid financial collapse caused by the high cost of nursing home care. But like any insurance, the legal contract provisions can be somewhat misleading.

Here are some legal provisions to watch for with LTC insurance:

- How does the policy define "nursing home care"? There are several levels: skilled, intermediate, and custodial. Medicare covers only skilled care. Will the policy pay if you need supervised living without technical medical help?

- What benefit does the policy provide? Most pay a fixed per-day rate. Will that be enough to cover the cost of care in your area?

- Does the policy adjust for inflation, or will the per-day rate pay for less-and-less as care becomes more expensive?

- Does the policy require you to be in the hospital for a certain number of days before admission to the nursing home? Some of the newer policies are doing away with that pre-hospitalization requirement, while others are so restrictive they'll only pay for nursing home care that is a follow-up to hospitalization.

- Most policies contain a waiting period before they will pay. The first 20 (or more) days of care have to come out of your pocket even though you've paid for the LTC insurance. The less days you pay for, the better the policy.

- Most policies will not pay the bills for any illness you had before you bought the policy; some have a waiting period of up to 2 years before they begin to pay. The shortest wait is the best. Also, many policies will not pay the bills if you contract a mental or nervous

condition, unless there is a direct physical
cause (as with Alzheimer's disease).

Look for a policy where the legal contract provisions:

- include guaranteed renewability (they cannot cancel so long as you pay the premiums);

- waive payment of the premium after you enter a nursing home; and

- include a flat premium that does not increase as you get older.

Medicaid

When a loved family member enters a nursing home,
qualifying for Medicaid can be a matter of survival. But
Medicaid is not available to everyone. Because it is a
welfare program, much of its funding is spent on providing medical care to dependent children, disabled persons,
and the poor.

To qualify for Medicaid funds for nursing care, four tests
must be met:

- Age (the patient must be over age 65);

- Level of Care (the patient must need skilled or intermediate care -- "custodial care" will not be provided);

- Income must be low enough; and

    ◆   Assets must not exceed legal limits.

Income Test

An individual's income cannot exceed $1,221 per month, and a couple's income cannot exceed $2,442 per month. If your income is even one dollar over the limit, Medicaid will not pay a penny for your care.

The income limit is raised from time to time. Generally, when social security benefits go up, so does the income limit. Check with your local Medicaid authority for an update.

Asset Limitation Test

Your assets are categorized by Medicaid as either "countable" or "exempt." All assets not exempt are "countable," and if countable assets exceed $2000 value for a single person or $3000 for a married couple, Medicaid will not pay for nursing home care.

An individual's exempt assets include:

1. $1500 in life insurance or an earmarked burial fund (but not both),

2. $4500 value in an automobile,

3. a burial plot, regardless of its value, and

4. the homestead.

A married couple's exempt assets include all of the above, plus a "spousal impoverishment" allowance of either $12,000 or 1/2 of your countable resources up to $60,000, whichever is greater.

The larges exemption is for your homestead: the full value of your home (whether $10,000 or $500,000) is exempt. But there is an important condition: your home is exempt only if you express an *intent* to return to it if you are able to leave the nursing home, or if your spouse or a dependent continues to reside there.

Before you go to the nursing home, you (or your spouse or dependent) must have lived in the home you claim as exempt. You cannot claim any other type of real estate as an exemption.

The exemption relies on your intentions, not your abilities. It does not matter that you may be too incapacitated to actually return to your home. Therefore, you should think long and hard before deciding that you will never go home again.

Medicaid Planning

Medicaid Planning involves manipulating your resources so the government will pay part of the cost of your health care.

The issue is who should pay for your health care: you or the government? Feelings run high in favor of both answers.

Medicaid is generally considered a welfare program, intended to assist low-income, low-asset citizens. But by pre-planning, some people with more resources have been able to qualify.

The concept utilizes existing Medicaid laws. For example: John has a modest income of $975 per month and has a tract of land he inherited from his uncle, worth $8000. The tract is an excess countable resource, and disqualifies him from receiving Medicaid.

If John gives away the tract, he will be disqualified from Medicaid assistance for 4 months, and will then begin to receive benefits.

The rule is: if you give away a "countable" resource, the value of that resource determines the length of time you are disqualified from receiving Medicaid benefits, up to 30 months. If nursing care costs $2,000/month in this area and you give away an $8,000 resource, you are disqualified from benefits for 4 months ($8,000 divided by $2,000 = 4).

There is little controversy when people in John's position use existing rules to qualify for assistance.

More controversy arises when people with amounts greatly exceeding the resource limits use the same technique. For instance: George has a $250,000 C.D. which produces around $1,700/month income. It becomes clear that George needs nursing home care, so he gives his C.D. to his daughter as a gift.

Under the rules, George is disqualified from receiving Medicaid assistance for the maximum 30 month period. He (or his daughter) will have to pay out of pocket $60,000 for nursing care ($2000/month for 30 months). After that, Medicaid will pay for his care.

George has protected $190,000 for his family by causing Medicaid to pay for his care after the 30th month.

Some people feel that George's actions are wrong. Others feel that is actions were legal and therefor he was entitled to save his assets. You'll have to decide what you would do in similar circumstances.

Spousal Protection Rules

A provision of the Medicare Catastrophic Coverage Act (MCCA) still exists, although overall it was repealed. The surviving portion deals with Medicaid, the "welfare" medical program intended for those who cannot afford their own medical coverage.

The surviving provision of MCCA protects healthy spouses from "spousal impoverishment." It applies to any married couple, one of whom was in a nursing home on or after September 30, 1989, for any period longer than 29 days.

Medicaid will not pay for nursing home care unless the applicant qualifies. To qualify, you must have a relatively small income and you must have very few assets. This provision caused many families to lose their life savings when catastrophic illness struck, leaving the healthy spouse with no means of support. But the surviving provision of MCCA provides some protection to the healthy spouse. The protection works as follows:

First, a "snapshot" of the couples asset value is taken. The valued is fixed at midnight of the first day of the month in which the ill spouse enters the nursing home.

Second, the value of the following items is subtracted (meaning that they are protected assets over-and-above the spousal impoverishment exemption): pre-paid burial contracts, household items, one automobile, and the home.

Third, an exemption is granted to the healthy spouse for ½ of the value, but not less than $12,000 or more than $60,000. Everything else is viewed as a resource of the ill spouse, and is counted against the ill spouse's ability to qualify for Medicaid.

For example, Carl and Elizabeth are married. On March 1, Carl entered a nursing home. They have a house (valued at $70,000), a certificate of deposit (valued at $20,000) and stocks and bonds (valued at $30,000). The house is not included in the calculations, but the C.D. and stock value of $50,000 is part of the "snapshot" taken on March 1. One half of $50,000, or $25,000 is set aside as Elizabeth's share.

Carl's $25,000 share is too much to allow him to get Medicaid, so it must be spent on medical care. At $2,000 per month, he is able to pay for 12-½ months of care. After that time, Carl's application for Medicaid will be approved. Elizabeth will still have $25,000 cash and a $70,000 house to care for her own needs. Poverty will be avoided.

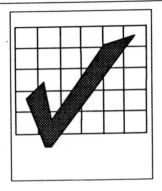

Chapter 16: Medicare

Administration

Medi*care* is different from, but almost as complex as Medic*aid.* Medicare is the U.S. nationalized medicine program, created in the 1960s, and still operating much the same way today.

Where Medicaid is administered by each state, Medicare is administered by the Health Care Finance Administration (HCFA), a branch of the federal government. HCFA enters into contracts with "intermediaries" (insurance companies) to do much of the paperwork and daily tasks required by Medicare. Blue Cross & Blue Shield of Texas is the intermediary you are most likely to encounter.

Medicare Part A Coverage

Part A covers social security and railroad retirement recipients after they reach age 65. No other qualifications need be met. Certain other groups, like dependents and persons with end-stage renal disease (kidney failure) are covered as well.

Part A is hospitalization insurance. It pays for your care based on HCFA's pre-determination of what care should cost (not on the actual cost of services rendered). The pre-determined cost is categorized by "Diagnostic Related Group," called DRGs. When a claim is made for payment by a hospital, the Intermediary looks at a book listing the DRGs, finds the patient's illness, and pays a set rate for that illness.

Because the hospital is paid a set rate, it wants you out as soon as possible. The longer your stay, the less profit it derives from your visit. The shorter your stay, the more profit, which is why hospitals often seem to "push patients out the door."

Under those restrictions, here is what Medicare pays for:

- **Inpatient Hospital Services.** Bed and board, nursing, hospital facilities, medical social services, pharmaceuticals and supplies used while in the hospital, and the services of some hospital interns or residents.

Medicare pays for the first 60 days of these services in full, except for the required deductible, during each "spell of illness." The deductible, modified regularly, is $592 (1991).

A "spell of illness" (sometimes called a benefit period) starts when you enter the hospital and ends 60 days after you go home. So, if you go to the hospital for 20 days, then go home for 30 days, then go back to the hospital (even for an unrelated condition) you are in the same "spell of illness." If you go to the hospital for 20 days, go home for 70 days, then go back to the hospital, you are in a new spell of illness and your benefits are renewed.

If hospitalized for more than 60 days, then during the 61st to 90th day of a spell of illness the patient must contribute $194 per day to the cost of the services.

After the 90th day, the patient may draw against an additional 60-day lifetime reserve. These reserve days can be used only once in a lifetime, and during them the patient must contribute $298 per day to the cost of care.

♦ **Post-Hospitalization Nursing Home Care** if the level of care required is "skilled." Never count on receiving this benefit -- it is granted on a highly limited basis. When granted, it partially covers nursing and rehabilitation costs for up to 100 days.

Qualifying for Medicare's nursing home coverage requires that you spend three days in the hospital (not including the day of discharge). It also requires that you be sent to the nursing home on doctor's orders within 30 days of the day you leave the hospital.

Further, only the first 20 days of care are fully paid for by Medicare. After that, the patient must contribute approximately $74 per day.

♦ **Home health care services.** These services are more liberal today than ever. The benefits can be very useful. Medicare will cover the entire cost of part-time skilled nursing care at home, or of physical, speech or occupational therapy at home when prescribed by a physician. It will not pay for drugs, full-time nursing care, home delivered meals, or housekeeping services.

To qualify, the patient must be home bound or in an institution which is not a hospital or skilled nursing facility. The patient's doctor must prescribe and monitor the services, which must be provided by a qualified home health services agency.

You do not need to be hospitalized before you can ask for these benefits.

♦ **Hospice services.** When the patient is diagnosed as terminal, Medicare will pay for the full cost of hospice care received in the home.

This includes all fees for nursing care charged by the Medicare-approved hospice provider. It may also include part of the cost of pain medications, short-term hospitalization and counselling.

Medicare Part B: Physician's Services

Medicare Part B is optional and a premium must be paid to purchase the coverage. It is designed to cover part of the cost of physician's care, outpatient care, therapy, and even some drugs.

All bills for services must be submitted to the Intermediary (usually Blue Cross & Blue Shield) by the care provider. The Intermediary will pay 80% of what it decides is reasonable for that care. The patient pays the rest.

Part B pays for physician's services -- the surgeon, anesthesiologist, etc. It also pays for medical supplies and drugs deemed medically necessary and which cannot be self-administered. It pays for lab work and x-rays while you are in the hospital. Part B also pays for prosthetics (artificial limbs), dialysis and certain vaccines.

The list of items Part B will not cover is almost as important as the list of items it will. Part B will NOT pay for:

- Routine physical exams
- Eyeglasses or contact lenses, or eye exams
- Hearing aids or hearing exams
- Routine immunizations
- Any type of custodial care (feeding, dressing, washing)
- Dental services
- Cosmetic surgery
- Routine foot care and orthopedic shoes
- Routine diagnostic testing and lab work (unless hospitalized)
- Prescription drugs that can be self-administered (like pills, ointments and insulin), and
- Certain outpatient physical therapy, x-rays and ambulance services.

This exclusion list is the main reason for the booming Medi-Gap insurance market.

Medi-Gap Policies

Medicare Supplement Insurance Policies, commonly called Medi-Gap policies, are tightly regulated by the Texas State Board of Insurance. The Board publishes a useful guide, "Shopper's Guide to Medicare Supplement Insurance in Texas," which compares all the policies offered by insurance companies in Texas.

You should only need ONE medi-gap policy, if any. If you qualify for Medicaid (and Medicare) a medi-gap policy should not be necessary. If your employer offers group health coverage then your needs may also be met. Keep your money if possible.

By law, you get a 30-day "free-look" at any medi-gap policy. Even after you agree to purchase the policy and pay the first premium, the company must allow you to cancel and give you a refund during the first 30-day period. If you do return the policy, send it to the insurance company by certified mail so you'll have a record of the date.

Here are the list of items to compare when shopping for a medi-gap policy:

1. Will it pay your Medicare Part A deductible?

2. Will it pay your Medicare Part B deductible?

3. Will it pay the cost difference between Medicare's reimbursement for medical care and what the doctor actually charges?

4. Will it pay for out-of-hospital prescription drugs?

5. Will it pay for a private duty nurse while you are in the hospital?

6. Is it guaranteed to be renewable, even though you make a claim?

7. How long is the waiting period before it will pay for an illness you already had before buying the policy?

8. Will it pay for any nursing home care?

Chapter 17: Property Protection

Homestead: Urban and Rural

Homestead protection is cherished by Texans. Our homes are legally protected by the Texas Constitution from seizure to pay debts.

There are two types of homestead: urban and rural. If your home is served by municipal utilities, police and fire protection (whether or not you are actually located within city limits) then you have an Urban Homestead. A Rural Homestead is in a place that does not receive those municipal services.

Legally an urban homestead can include up to one acre of land and improvements. A rural homestead is defined similarly as up to 200 acres with improvements if you are married, or up to 100 acres with improvements if you are single.

Protection & Limits

The Texas Constitution and Texas Property Code make your homestead legally exempt from claims of creditors. If, for example, you get into a dispute over payment of a large bill and the creditor obtains a court judgment requiring you to pay, the creditor cannot collect against your homestead.

Protection of your homestead is not, however, universal. Law allows your homestead to be taken in four situations:

1. Your mortgage company can foreclose if you fail to pay back the money you borrowed to purchase your home or money you borrowed to improve your home.

2. The federal or local government can take your home for failure to pay taxes. As to Texas property taxes, there is specific protection for those over age 65: your home cannot be taken for failure to pay Texas property taxes if you have filed for a deferral of tax or abatement of collection. A federal tax lien (by the IRS) is

not affected by the Texas deferral or abatement procedure.

3. A contractor can foreclose if you fail to pay for improvements to your home. The contractor must, however, properly create his "mechanics and materialmens lien" against your home. You and your spouse must both agree to the lien in writing before work is started or materials are furnished. You must also be given a specific written warning in the contract that failure to follow its terms may result in the loss of your home.

4. You can forfeit homestead protection by abandonment of the homestead. If you surrender your rights by walking away from your homestead, creditors can take it. However, you do not surrender your rights simply because of prolonged absence (especially if you express an intent to return to your home). Texas court decisions also state that lengthy absence from home due to illness is not considered abandonment of your homestead.

Tax Deferral on Homestead

Texas allows residents over 65 to defer payment of property taxes on their homestead. This includes school, county and city taxes. It does not include any federal tax collected by the IRS. The law also allows abatement of a lawsuit to collect a delinquent property tax on your homestead.

"Defer" means delay payment. The taxes are still owed by you or your estate: payment is just delayed until your homestead loses its homestead character because you sell, move out or die.

Getting the deferral is simple. You must obtain "Form 33.06" from your local Tax Appraisal District.

The required form must be signed by you in front of a notary. You will need to know the legal description of your home. You need to swear that you are 65 or older and that the described property is occupied by you as your homestead.

Filing for deferral or abatement does not mean you no longer owe the taxes. The collection authority can still place a lien against your home, but cannot act to enforce it. Also, while interest will accrue while you owe outstanding taxes, penalties are waived.

House Bill 421, effective September 1989, waived imposition of all penalties during a valid property tax deferral period, but the taxes and interest are still due. Although a tax lien may remain on the property and interest continues to accrue, a penalty many not be imposed during a deferral period.

In this context, "defer" means you can forestall the filing of a collection lawsuit until you no longer own and occupy the house. To defer collection, you must file form 33.06 with the Appraisal District any time before collection action is begun.

"Abate" means to stop an already existing collection suit. You must file form 33.06 with the court that would hear the lawsuit. The tax authority may try to disprove your right to an abatement, but the final decision is the Judge's. If no objection is raised by the tax authority, the lawsuit is suspended until you no longer own and occupy the homestead property.

The deferral and abatement procedure is made available to those over 65 to help if you do not have enough money to pay your property taxes. The procedure is another way Texas law tries to make your senior years easier.

Personal Property Exemption

Question:

My husband and I are retired on a fixed income. We need our assets to last as long as possible. The biggest fear we have is of being sued for some type of accident and losing everything. We have insurance, but with the huge judgments we read about, who knows if it will be enough if something were to happen? Is there any legal limit to judgments in Texas or can they take everything away?

Answer:

Texas law provides two types of shelters against legal liability: the homestead exemption and the personal property exemption. This is less well known but very important.

The personal property exemption shelters your personal necessities. On May 24, 1991 an amendment to this law expanded its coverage. It forbids the authorities from seizing, garnishing, attaching, or executing against a very specific list of items -- even to satisfy a court judgment.

Under the expanded law, a family is allowed to shelter assets with a market value up to $60,000. A single adult is limited to $30,000 value. These limits represent a doubling of the protection granted by the old law, which allowed only $30,000 for a family or $15,000 for a single adult.

Over and above the $60,000 limit, the law forbids the authorities from seizing your current wages and from seizing "professionally prescribed health aids." This means that if you have special medical equipment in your home for an ill family member, the equipment is exempt from seizure regardless of its value.

If a judgment is entered against you, you must be given the opportunity to set aside assets valued up to $60,000. You are allowed to chose any combination from the following items:

- home furnishings and family heirlooms
- foodstuffs
- tools, equipment, books and vehicles used in your trade
- farm or ranch vehicles, implements, and some livestock
- clothing
- jewelry (so long as it does not exceed $15,000 in value)
- two guns (remember, this is *Texas* law)
- car for each driving member of the family
- athletic equipment, and
- life insurance.

The combination of personal items you select from the above list cannot exceed $60,000 in value. On top of that, your homestead is protected without regard to any monetary limit. So even though there is no limit to the possible size of a court judgment, you are certain that you will never be stripped of the necessities of life.

Chapter 18: Your Drivers License

Revocation of License

Question:

My husband is diabetic and when he doesn't eat just right he can "black-out" for short periods of time. Twice he blacked-out while driving, but no one was hurt and there was no property damage. Now he's gotten notice from the Department of Public Safety that his driver's license is being revoked. Can they do that?

Answer:

Your driver's license is precious to you because it provides you independence. But your independence must be weighed against other precious essentials: life and safety.

An automobile can be dangerous in the wrong hands. The old adage that "driving is a privilege, not a right" is generally true. In order to drive, you must have a driver's license. In order to get and keep a driver's license, you must meet the requirements of Texas law.

Article 6687b of the Texas Statutes regulates issuance and revocation of a driver's license. By law, a driver's license may be revoked if:

◆   a person is found by a Court to be incompetent (which means that if Guardianship is granted over you, you can no longer drive), or

◆   a person is, in the opinion of the Department of Public Safety (DPS), unable to "exercise reasonable and ordinary care" while driving due to physical or mental disability.

How do they find out about your disability? You are supposed to reveal to DPS, when you apply for a license renewal, any medical condition that might hamper your ability to drive safely. This may be used against you later.

Texas law has created a Medical Advisory Board to assist the DPS with physical or mental disability decisions. The

Board can call together local panels of medical experts to review medical records and examinations. Based on this study, the local panels advise DPS on your mental or physical abilities.

If the panel decides your disabilities make your driving unsafe, your license can be revoked or suspended. The panel can require you to submit to a medical examination. Refusal to submit to a required examination is grounds for revoking your driver's license, whether or not you have any physical disabilities that make your driving dangerous.

The final say in the revocation process comes from your local Justice of the Peace or Municipal Judge. If all the evidence indicates your driving is dangerous, the Judge will revoke your license. The safety of pedestrians and other motorists must come first.

Transportation alternatives include mass transit, taxi-cabs, senior centers, and senior transportation. Your local area agency on aging can provide details of other transportation services available in your area. Call the Texas Department on Aging (they are listed in the "Resources" chapter) for information about your local area agency on aging.

Remember: when it comes to driving, there's more at stake than independence. Your health and safety and that of people on the road with you needs to come first.

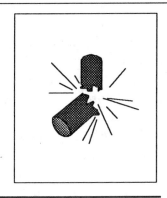

Chapter 19: Divorce in the Family

Grandparent's Rights

Question: Our son is getting a divorce. We never have gotten along well with our daughter-in-law, and we're afraid she will refuse to let us see our two grandchildren. What can we do?

Answer:

When your child gets a divorce, you and your grandchildren may be innocently caught in the cross-fire. You have limited rights as a grandparent. (To avoid confusion let's call you the "grandparent" and your child getting the divorce the "parent.")

In divorce, a Judge decides who gets custody and visitation of your grandchildren. Ordinarily, your son will become either "managing conservator" (and keep the grandchildren most of the time) or "possessory conservator" (and have pre-defined visitation rights). If your son will share the grandchildren during his time, that may satisfy you.

If you fear that neither parent will allow access to your grandchild, the Texas Family Code allows the Judge to grant you "reasonable access" to your grandchildren.

You can make your request for access before or after the divorce is final. It is more efficient to request access before the divorce is final, but it happens less frequently because problems usually have not begun yet.

After the divorce is final, you can request a "modification" of the divorce decree listing the specifics of your access rights. Intervening in "your children's concerns" may be hard, so you need to focus on meeting the needs of the grandchildren.

You must hire an attorney to assist. Look for one with extensive family law background. Discuss legal fees and court costs up-front to avoid surprises.

For you to get access, the "parent" must be the "biological or adoptive parent" of your grandchild. This means that if you are the step-grandparents from a second marriage the Court will not allow access unless your child officially adopted the grandchildren after marrying their natural parent.

The Judge must agree that allowing you to have access to the grandchildren is in their "best interest."

Although grandparents usually seek a court order ensuring access to the grandchildren when the parents are getting divorced, you may also do so if:

- the parent is in jail or incompetent;

- the parents are separated for 3 months or more;

- the parents are abusing the grandchild, or

- if the grandchild has resided with you for 6 out of the last 24 months.

How Divorce Affects Your Will

Question:

I was divorced from my husband in 1985. When we divorced, our house was left in both our names but only I lived there. His 1965 Last Will and Testament named me as heir and executrix. He died in 1988. Now someone claiming that my husband owed him money has gone to Probate Court. Doesn't my ex-husband's Will protect me?

Answer:

Your former husband may have believed that his 1965 Will could protect you, but it does not. Under the Texas Probate Code, when you get divorced any provision in a Last Will and Testament written before the divorce giving any assets to the former spouse is void. Also, any provision making the former spouse Executor is void.

Your ex-husband could have written a new Will after your divorce. The new Will would have over-ridden the Probate Code to put you in control.

His 1965 Will cannot protect you from the creditor. However, Texas' homestead laws forbid the creditor from collecting his debt against your ex-husband's interest in your house until a time when it is no longer your homestead.

Will provisions leaving assets to a spouse do not become void until divorce is final. If you die before the divorce is final, your spouse still inherits. If you are in the process of getting an unfriendly divorce, you should modify your Last Will and Testament immediately to remove your spouse.

Common Law Marriage

Question:

I am widowed for several years and have recently moved in with a man. We don't want to be married because that would affect our income. What is "common law marriage" and how does it happen?

Answer:

Common law marriage is the valid legal relationship of two people as husband and wife. It happens when two people agree to be married, then live together as husband and wife and tell other people that they are married. No specific amount of time need pass.

No ceremony takes place and no license is issued, so proving the existence of the marriage can be difficult. If you stood to gain by being married, you could file a "declaration of informal marriage" with the county clerk. If you stand to lose by being married, then never "agree" that you are married and never tell anyone else that you are married.

Chapter 20: Estate Tax Basics

There are many complexities in the estate tax system, but two particular opportunities for reducing taxes will affect most people.

Unlimited Marital Deduction

The Unlimited Marital Deduction eliminates estate tax on ALL assets passing to your surviving spouse. There is no dollar limit on the deduction. However, it must be used correctly to avoid bumping the survivor's estate into a higher tax bracket.

For example: Joe and Edna, married for 46 years, have acquired a joint estate of $350,000. When Joe dies, he leaves the entire amount to Edna. She does not pay any tax on the transfer, because the Unlimited Marital Deduction eliminates the tax.

Unified Credit

The Unified Credit eliminates estate or gift taxes on up to $600,000 of assets passing to anyone other than your surviving spouse. This is equivalent to a tax credit of $192,800. You can use the credit either while you are alive (by giving a gift larger than your annual $10,000 gift tax exclusion) or upon your death (by giving inheritances).

Each person is entitled to a Unified Credit. Husband has a $600,000 credit; Wife has a $600,000 credit. The key to proper use of the credit is for both spouses to use it to avoid estate or gift taxes.

Avoiding Estate Tax

By carefully combining the two rules every estate smaller than $1.2 million can avoid estate taxes. Let's look at an example:

Case 1:

John and Mary have assets of $800,000. They have wills leaving all assets to the surviving mate. When John dies, the Unlimited Marital Deduction eliminates the 30% estate tax on the transfer. When Mary dies (owning her

$400,000 and John's $400,000) the estate tax bracket is 33%. Mary's Unified Credit of $192,800 reduces the estate tax to $75,000. Hence, 9.4% of the assets are paid in taxes.

Case 2:

John and Mary's wills contain "Credit Shelter Trusts." When John dies, his assets are left to the trust for Mary's benefit. His Unified Credit eliminates the 30% estate tax on the transfer. When Mary dies, her estate is $400,000 (because John's half went to the trust). Her Unified Credit eliminates all estate tax. Hence, none of the assets are paid in taxes.

By using the Credit Shelter Trust, John and Mary saved $75,000. Larger estates save even more, but estates above $1.2 million can use other tax saving techniques as well.

Using the Unified Credit in both estates can save considerable money, since estate tax rates are the highest of any federal tax. It makes sense to reduce the tax in any way the law allows.

Step Up in Basis

Basis is the dollar figure the IRS uses when determining income tax on the sale of a piece of property. For instance, if you bought 200 shares of AT&T in 1950 for $8 per share, your basis is $8 per share (unless it is adjusted by the IRS for depreciation or other reasons). When you sell the stock in 1992 for $60 per share, your taxable gain is only that part of the sale price which was more than your basis (that is $60 - $8 = $52 gain). Your basis is like your "investment."

When you inherit an asset, what is that asset's income tax basis? The answer is: the fair market value of that asset on the day the owner died.

Using the AT&T example: if the fair market value of the stock on the day the owner died was $60, then your inherited basis in the stock is $60. If you sell it the next day for $60 per share, you pay no capital gains tax. This can add up to significant savings when applied to many assets.

The step up in basis rule provides an added benefit in Community Property states: when your spouse dies, you get to use the higher basis for the inheritance and for the half of the Community Property estate you already owned.

'QTIP' Trust Planning

Question:

I remarried after the death of my first wife. We both have children from our earlier marriages. Is there any way I can plan to protect my current wife after I die, yet have my children get my estate after her death?

Answer:

Most people want to protect their spouse financially after their death. But if you are in a second marriage, you may be wary that "her kids" will benefit ahead of "your kids" when she dies. And naturally you want to keep estate taxes low.

How can these goals be achieved? Try leaving your assets to a trust designed to benefit your spouse, then pay the remainder to "your kids" when your spouse dies. Although an ordinary gift to your spouse is estate tax free, a limitation like leaving assets to your spouse only until her death is not tax free unless the "QTIP" rules are followed.

"QTIP" stands for Qualified Terminable Interest Property. "Terminable" means that ownership stops with the passage of time or on some particular event (like the death of your spouse). However, "qualified" means that the gift is estate tax free anyway.

Federal law allows "terminable interests" to qualify for favorable tax treatment if these conditions are met:

- the spouse must receive all income from the assets, payable at least annually;

- ♦ no one may have a "power of appointment" (the ability to give away the property); and

- ♦ the Executor must timely notify the IRS that the assets are being treated as QTIP assets.

Here's an example:

Richard and Gwen each have children from earlier marriages. Richard wants to protect Gwen (his second wife) but wants "his kids" to get his assets after Gwen dies. Richard makes a Last Will and Testament placing his assets into a QTIP trust when he dies. All income will be paid to Gwen, at least annually. Richard's Will says that when Gwen dies, the assets must go directly to his son Steven.

The trust is a "terminable interest" because Gwen's benefits end when she dies. But it is "qualified," since Gwen gets the income her whole life. The assets pass without estate tax and both the wife and child have been protected.

Chapter 21: Notaries & Legal Advice

Whose Advice Do I Take?

Question:

My Will was prepared by a Notary Public in 1973. After doing some reading on my own, I noticed that some important legal points may be missing from my Will. Why did the Notary do it wrong? Aren't Notaries supposed to help with legal documents?

Answer:

Never rely on a Notary Public to prepare any legal document. Texas law states that a Notary Public may only notarize written documents, administer oaths, and make certified copies of documents which cannot be publicly recorded (like letters or business accounts).

To become a Notary, one need only apply to the Texas Secretary of State, pay the required filing fee, and purchase a suitable bond. A Notary commission from the Secretary of State does not qualify a person to write your Will.

Notaries do not have any special training. On the other hand, to become a licensed attorney in Texas a person must graduate from college, graduate from law school, and pass the Texas bar exam. A notary faces no educational requirements.

Being a notary does not allow a person to practice law. Only lawyers can practice law, which includes writing wills, deeds, contracts, and powers of attorney. A Notary is legally forbidden to practice law unless that Notary is also a licensed lawyer.

Since your Will was illegally prepared by a Notary, many important legal provisions may have been left out. Does your Will include:

- Appointment of an Independent Executor and backup executors if your first choice cannot take office?

- Waiver of the bond requirement for your Executor?

- ◆ Properly worded bequests of your assets, and backup recipients if your first choices are not alive to receive your bounty?

- ◆ The date you signed it, your signature, and signatures of at least 2 witnesses?

- ◆ A Self Proving Affidavit so that the witnesses do not have to appear in court?

Some of the confusion comes from Texas's Mexican origins. In Mexico, a *notario publico* must also be a lawyer and must have a law degree. In Texas, it is illegal for the phrase *notario publico* to be used by a notary. It is misleading, and is considered a "deceptive trade practice."

When notaries act within statutory authority (that is, notarize a document, administer an oath, or certify a copy) they are indispensable. But you should take your Will to a licensed attorney for review and modification. Never rely on a notary for legal advice.

Chapter 22: Volunteer Liability

Protection by Law

Question:

My church runs an all-volunteer center to provide assistance to sick people in our neighborhood. Some of the volunteers have been wondering if they will be legally protected from liability if something goes wrong. Is there any legal protection for volunteers in Texas?

Answer:

Yes, if all of the qualifications are met. In the mid-1980's the legislature got the message that volunteers, in fear of liability, were staying home. The Texas

Charitable Immunity and Liability Act was passed in 1987 as an antidote.

The Act partly limits a volunteer's liability. "Volunteers" are people who work for an organization without being paid (except for expense reimbursement). "Employees" are not volunteers because they get paid by the organization.

A volunteer is legally protected and immune from civil liability for any act or omission, even if it results in someone's death, or injury, or in property damage if the mishap occurred while the volunteer was "acting in the course and scope" of his duties for the organization. He must also be acting "in good faith" in order to be immune. Good Faith means "honest pursuit" of the activities the organization was created to provide.

Volunteers are not protected from liability if:

- an injury results from a volunteer's intentional, willful or wantonly negligent act; or

- an injury results from an act done with conscious disregard for the safety of others.

If the mishap occurs while the volunteer is operating a vehicle the volunteer is legally liable but only up to the level covered by existing insurance. Texas law requires all vehicle operators to have liability insurance with the following limits: $20,000 for injury or death of one person, $40,000 for injury or death of two people, and

$15,000 for property damage arising out of any one accident.

Even though you are a volunteer, your liability is only limited if the organization you help is "qualified" by being either:

- ◆ a registered tax-exempt organization under the Internal Revenue Code;

- ◆ a homeowners' association; or

- ◆ an organization that provides charitable or religious services, prevents cruelty to animals or children, provides youth sports or recreation, provides educational services, or (more generally) provides for the social welfare and common good of the people in a community. The organization must also meet other conditions such as refraining from political activities.

The organization must also have adequate liability insurance. Law requires the organization to carry liability insurance that covers $1,000,000 for personal injury and $100,000 for property damage. If it fails to do so, then the organization and its employees do not have immunity (but the volunteers are still safe).

Make sure the organization with which you volunteer meets all the legally required conditions. When it does, you are legally protected.

Chapter 23: Resources

Valuable Resources

AARP
1909 K Street N.W.
Washington, D.C. 20049
202-728-4300

Area VII Office
8144 Walnut Hill Lane
Dallas, Texas
214-361-3060

Self Help: Legal Services for the Elderly
7410 Blanco Road, Suite 420
San Antonio, Texas 78216   512-366-2222

This legal services provider assists in preparation of certain legal documents on a set-fee basis, providing an inexpensive and fast way to obtain valid planning tools. Included are: Durable Powers of Attorney, Health Care Powers of Attorney, Directives to Physician, Declarations of Guardian, and Community Property Survivorship Agreements. Call or write to place an order.

Alzheimer's Association   800-523-2007 or

Austin   512-454-5476
Dallas   214-754-0085
El Paso   915-584-7881
Ft. Worth   817-926-8715
Houston   713-623-0796
San Antonio   512-523-2007

National Council on Aging
600 Maryland Ave., S.W.
Washington, D.C. 20024

Foundation for Hospice and Home Care
519 C Street N.E.
Washington, D.C. 20002

Geriatric Education Center
University of Texas Health Science Center
7703 Floyd Curl Drive
San Antonio, Texas 78248   512-567-3372

The G.E.C. in San Antonio is one of several federally funded resource centers for the elderly. They conduct classes for professionals and provide information for anyone in need. The G.E.C. can network to other areas of the U.S., so it is a useful starting point no matter where you are.

The Arthritis Foundation

Austin	512-451-7323
Fort Worth	817-926-7733
Houston	713-579-1700
San Antonio	800-284-2438

National Academy of Elder Law Attorneys
1730 E. River Road, Ste 107
Tucson, Az. 85718 602-881-4005

Nutrition Services

Texas Association of Nutrition and Aging Services
P.O. Box 1211, Orange, Texas 77630

Austin: City Wide Nutrition	800-635-4116
Dallas: Meals on Wheels	214-689-0000
El Paso: County Nutrition Project	915-532-2433
Ft. Worth: City Wide Nutrition	800-635-4116
Houston: City Wide Nutrition	713-523-1640
San Antonio: City Wide Nutrition	800-635-4116

Society for the Right to Die
250 W. 57th Street
New York, N.Y. 10107 212-246-6973

Legal Referrals & Assistance

Legal Hotline for Older Texans	800-622-2520
Austin: Travis County Bar Assn.	512-472-8303
Dallas: Legal Aid	214-742-7650

El Paso: Legal Assistance	915-544-3022
Ft. Worth: Tarrant County Bar Assn.	817-336-4101
Houston: Lawyer Referral	713-237-9429
San Antonio:	
Bexar County Bar Assn.	512-227-1853
Legal Assistance/Peer Counselling	512-733-1032
State Bar of Texas	800-252-9690

Texas Medical Association
1801 N. Lamar Blvd.
Austin, Texas 78701   512-477-6704

Senior Citizen Services

Austin Community Services	512-444-0511
Dallas Aging Information Office	214-741-5244
El Paso Services to Aged	915-775-4591
Ft. Worth Sr. Citizens Services	817-338-4433
Houston Sheltering Arms	713-524-6560
San Antonio Senior Services	512-227-3148

Parkinson's Disease Information

Houston	713-799-5970
Dallas	214-343-2315

American Society on Aging
833 Market Street
San Francisco, Ca. 94103   415-543-2617

National Council of Senior Citizens
925 15th St NW
Washington, D.C.   202-347-8800

Texas Toll-Free Hotlines

Comptroller of Public Accounts   800-252-5555
Make inquiries about taxes and organizations

Adult Protective Services   800-252-5400
Texas Department of Human Services
P.O. Box 149030, Austin, Tx. 78714

Fair Housing/Equal Opportunity   800-424-8590
Department of Housing and Urban Development

Texas Housing Discrimination   800-424-8590

Health Department   800-252-9106
Bureau of Long-term Care, State of Texas
To complaint about nursing facilities

Lawyer Referral   800-252-9690
State Bar of Texas

Legal Hotline for Older Texans   800-622-2520
Texas Legal Services Center, Austin

Medicare, Part B Information   800-442-2620
Information on claims and assistance

Medicare Eligibility & Information   800-234-5772

Medicaid Hotline   800-252-8263
Texas Department of Human Services

Medicaid Fraud & Patient Abuse   800-252-8011
Attorney General of Texas

Blue Cross & Blue Shield   800-442-2620
P.O. Box 660031, Dallas, Texas 75226

Texas State Library for the Blind   800-252-9605

Texas Department on Aging   800-252-9240
P.O. Box 12786, Austin, Tx 78711

Employment Discrimination   800-872-3362
Equal Employment Opportunity Commission

Texas Employment Commission   800-252-9924

Report Crime-Solving "Tips"   800-252-8477
Governor's Crime Stoppers Advisory Council

Crime Victim Assistance   800-252-3423

Federal Information Center   800-366-2998

Social Security   800-234-5772
Eligibility and information

Mental Health Services   800-252-8154
Department of Mental Health & Mental Retardation

Veteran's Complaints   800-368-5899
DVA Inspector General

TDD Operator   800-855-1155
Telephone Device for the Deaf

State Board of Insurance   800-252-3439
Complaints about policies and insurance agents

State Nursing Home Ombudsman   800-252-2412
Problems with Resident/Caregiver relationship

Appendix A

Sample Form: Health Care Power of Attorney

*This form is based upon Texas law,
pursuant to VATS Article 4590h-1.
It reads as follows:*

This is an important legal document. Before signing this document, you should know these important facts:

Except to the extent you state otherwise, this document gives the person you name as your agent the authority to make any and all health care decisions for you in accordance with your wishes, including your religious and moral beliefs, when you are no longer capable of making them yourself. Because "health care" means any treatment, service, or procedure to maintain, diagnose, or treat your physical or mental condition, your agent has the power to make a broad range of health care decisions for you. Your agent may consent, refuse to consent, or withdraw consent to medical treatment and may make decisions about withdrawing or withholding life-sustaining treatment. Your agent may *not* consent to voluntary inpatient mental health services, convulsive treatment, psychosurgery, or abortion. A physician must comply with your agent's instructions or allow you to be transferred to another physician.

Your agent's authority begins when your doctor certifies that you lack the capacity to make health care decisions.

Your agent is obligated to follow your instructions when making decisions on your behalf. Unless you state otherwise, your agent has the same authority to make decisions about your health care as you would have had.

It is important that you discuss this document with your physician or other health care provider before you sign it to make sure that you understand the nature and range of decisions that may be made on your behalf. If you do not have a physician, you should talk with someone else who is knowledgeable about these issues and can answer your questions. You do not need a lawyer's assistance to complete this document, but if there is anything in this document that you do not understand, you should ask a lawyer to explain it to you.

The person you appoint as agent should be someone you know and trust. The person must be 18 years of age or older or a person under 18 years of age who has had the disabilities of minority removed. If you appoint your health or residential care provider (*e.g.*, your physician or an employee of a home health agency, hospital, nursing home, or residential care home, other than a relative), that person has to choose between acting as your agent or as your health or residential care provider; the law does not permit a person to do both at the same time.

You should inform the person you appoint that you want the person to be your health care agent. You should discuss this document with your agent and your physician and give each a signed copy. You should indicate on the document itself the people and institutions who have signed copies. Your agent is not liable for health care decisions made in good faith on your behalf.

Even after you have signed this document, you have the right to make health care decisions for yourself as long as you are able to do so and treatment cannot be given to you or stopped over your objection. You have the right to revoke the authority granted to your agent by informing your agent or your health or residential care provider orally or in writing, or by you execution of a subsequent Durable Power of Attorney for health care. Unless you state otherwise, your appointment of a spouse dissolves on divorce.

This document may not be changed or modified. If you want to make changes in the document, you must make an entirely new one.

You may wish to designate an alternate agent in the event that your agent is unwilling, unable, or ineligible to act as your agent. Any alternate agent you designate has the same authority to make health care decisions for you.

This Power of Attorney is not valid unless it is signed in the presence of two or more qualified witnesses. The following persons may not act as witnesses:

1. the person you have designated as your agent;

2. your health or residential care provider or an employee of your health or residential care provider;

3. your spouse;

4. your lawful heirs or beneficiaries named in your Will or a deed; or

5. creditors or persons who have a claim against you.

Health Care Power of Attorney

---

1. Designation of Health Care Agent: I, John Smith, appoint the following person as my agent to make any and all health care decisions for me, except to the extent I state otherwise in this document:

Name: _____
Street: _____
City, State, Zip: _____
Telephone: _____

This Durable Power of Attorney for health care takes effect if I become unable to make my own health care decisions and this fact is certified in writing by my physician.

2. Limitations: I place the following limitations on the decision making authority of my agent, and no others:

_____
_____

3. Designation of Alternate Agent: You are not required to designate an alternate agent but you may do so. An alternate agent may make the same health care decisions as the designated agent if the desig-

nated agent is unable or unwilling to act as your agent. If the agent designated is your spouse, the designation is automatically revoked by law if your marriage is dissolved. If the person designated as my agent is unable or unwilling to make health care decisions for me, I designate the following persons to serve as my agent to make health care decisions for me as authorized by this document, who serve in the following order:

a.   First Alternate Agent:
Name: _____
Street: _____
City, State, Zip: _____
Telephone: _____

b.   Second Alternate Agent:
Name: _____
Street: _____
City, State, Zip: _____
Telephone: _____

4. The original of this document is kept at:

_____
_____

5. The following individuals or institutions have signed copies:

Name: _____
Street: _____
City, State, Zip: _____
Telephone: _____

6. Duration: I understand that this Power of Attorney exists indefinitely from the date I execute this document unless I establish a shorter time or revoke the

Power of Attorney. If I am unable to make health care decisions for myself when this Power of Attorney expires, the authority I have granted my agent continues to exist until the time I become able to make health care decisions for myself.

This Power of Attorney ends on the following date: _____, 19_____.
(Note: You are not required to declare a termination date).

7. Prior Designations Revoked: I revoke any prior Durable Power of Attorney for health care.

8. Acknowledgment of Disclosure Statement: I sign my name below to acknowledge that I have been provided with a disclosure statement explaining the effect of this document. I have read and understand the information contained in the disclosure statement.

John Smith
Principal

9. Execution of Power of Attorney: I sign my name to this Durable Power of Attorney for health care on _____, 19___ in Beaumont, Texas.

John Smith
Principal

STATEMENT OF WITNESSES: I declare under penalty of perjury that the principal has identified himself or herself to me, that the principal signed or acknowledged this Durable Power of Attorney in my presence, that I believe the principal to be of sound mind, that the principal has affirmed that the principal is aware of the nature of the document and is signing it voluntarily and free from duress, that the principal requested that I serve as witness to the principal's execution of this document, that I am not the person appointed as agent by this document, and that I am not a provider of health or residential care, an employee of a provider of health or residential care, the operator of a community care facility, or an employee of an operator of a health care facility. I declare that I am not related to the principal by blood, marriage, or adoption and that to the best of my knowledge I am not entitled to any part of the estate of the principal on the death of the principal under a Will or by operation of a law.

_____   _____
Witness Signature   Witness Signature

Appendix B

Sample Form: Declaration of Guardian

This document is based on Texas law, pursuant to Texas Probate Code Section 118A. It reads as follows:

I, Jane Doe, make' this Declaration of Guardian, to operate if the need for a Guardian for me later arises.

1. I designate John Smith to serve as Guardian of my person and estate, Ed Smythe to serve as the first alternate Guardian of my person and estate, and Bubba Water to serve as the second alternate Guardian of my person and estate.

2. If any Guardian or alternate Guardian dies, fails, or refuses to qualify, or resigns, the next named alternate Guardian shall succeed the prior named Guardian and become my Guardian.

3. I expressly disqualify the following persons from ever serving as Guardian of my person or of my Estate:
   > My former husband Fred Doe; and
   > My brother James Smythe.

Signed on November 19, 1991.

  Jane Doe   continued....
Declarant

Witness: _____
Witness: _____

Self Proving Affidavit: Before me, the undersigned authority, on this date personally appeared the Declarant Jane Doe, and _____ and _____ as witnesses, and all being duly sworn, Declarant said that the above instrument was his Declaration of Guardian and that he had made and executed it for the purposes therein expressed. The Witnesses declared to me that they are each 14 years of age or older, that they saw the Declarant sign the Declaration, that they signed the Declaration as Witnesses, and that the Declarant appeared to them to be of sound mind.

Jane Doe
Declarant

Witness: _____
Witness: _____

Subscribed and sworn to before me by Jane Doe and the Witnesses on November 19, 1991.

_____
Notary Public -- State of Texas

Index

Keep Up With The Latest Changes!

Unfortunately, the laws upon which this book is based are everchanging, and are subject to new interpretations by the courts.

Annually, Paul Premack will revise his Senior Texan Legal Guide to incorporate federal & state law requirements. Everything you need to know to stay well informed on the legal issues facing Senior Texans will be included. If you would like to be kept informed of any subsequent versions, send us your name, address and phone number or call us at (512) 366-2222.

The Premack Law Office
7410 Blanco Road, Suite 420
San Antonio, TX 78216